W9-COW-232

SUBSTANCE ABUSE

GENERAL EDITORS

Dale C. Garell, M.D.
Medical Director, California Children Services, Department of Health Services,
    County of Los Angeles
Associate Dean for Curriculum; Clinical Professor, Department of Pediatrics &
    Family Medicine, University of Southern California School of Medicine
Former President, Society for Adolescent Medicine

Solomon H. Snyder, M.D.
Distinguished Service Professor of Neuroscience, Pharmacology, and Psychiatry,
    Johns Hopkins University School of Medicine
Former President, Society for Neuroscience
Albert Lasker Award in Medical Research, 1978

CONSULTING EDITORS

Robert W. Blum, M.D., Ph.D.
Professor and Director, Division of General Pediatrics and Adolescent Health,
    University of Minnesota

Charles E. Irwin, Jr., M.D.
Professor of Pediatrics; Director, Division of Adolescent Medicine, University of
    California, San Francisco

Lloyd J. Kolbe, Ph.D.
Director of the Division of Adolescent and School Health, Center for Chronic
    Disease Prevention and Health Promotion, Centers for Disease Control

Jordan J. Popkin
Former Director, Division of Federal Employee Occupational Health, U.S. Public
    Health Service Region I

Joseph L. Rauh, M.D.
Professor of Pediatrics and Medicine, Adolescent Medicine, Children's Hospital
    Medical Center, Cincinnati
Former President, Society for Adolescent Medicine

THE ENCYCLOPEDIA OF
H E A L T H

MEDICAL DISORDERS
AND THEIR TREATMENT

Dale C. Garell, M.D. · General Editor

SUBSTANCE ABUSE

William J. Hermes

Introduction by C. Everett Koop, M.D., Sc.D.
former Surgeon General, U. S. Public Health Service

CHELSEA HOUSE PUBLISHERS

New York · Philadelphia

The goal of the ENCYCLOPEDIA OF HEALTH *is to provide general information in the ever-changing areas of physiology, psychology, and related medical issues. The titles in this series are not intended to take the place of the professional advice of a physician or other health care professional.*

CHELSEA HOUSE PUBLISHERS
EDITOR-IN-CHIEF   Richard S. Papale
EXECUTIVE MANAGING EDITOR   Karyn Gullen Browne
COPY CHIEF   Philip Koslow
PICTURE EDITOR   Adrian G. Allen
ART DIRECTOR   Nora Wertz
MANUFACTURING DIRECTOR   Gerald Levine
SYSTEMS MANAGER   Lindsey Ottman
PRODUCTION COORDINATOR   Marie Claire Cebrián-Ume

BC 6113823

The Encyclopedia of Health
SENIOR EDITOR   Kenneth W. Lane

Staff for SUBSTANCE ABUSE
COPY EDITOR   Margaret Dornfeld
EDITORIAL ASSISTANT   Laura Petermann
PICTURE RESEARCHER   Sandy Jones
DESIGNER   Robert Yaffe

3 5 7 9 8 6 4 2

Library of Congress Cataloging-in-Publication Data

Substance abuse/by William Hermes; introduction by C. Everett Koop.
  p. cm.—(The Encyclopedia of health)
Includes bibliographical references and index.
Summary: Examines such substances as prescription drugs, marijuana, psychedelics, and heroin, discusses their functions and effects, and describes substance addiction and methods of treatment.
  ISBN 0-7910-0078-8
     0-7910-0506-2 (pbk.)
  1. Substance abuse—Juvenile literature. 2. Drug abuse—Juvenile literature. [1. Drugs. 2. Drug abuse.] I. Title. II. Series.   92-1625
RC564.3.H47 1993   CIP
616.86—dc20   AC

CONTENTS

THE ENCYCLOPEDIA OF
HEALTH

THE HEALTHY BODY

The Circulatory System
Dental Health
The Digestive System
The Endocrine System
Exercise
Genetics & Heredity
The Human Body: An Overview
Hygiene
The Immune System
Memory & Learning
The Musculoskeletal System
The Nervous System
Nutrition
The Reproductive System
The Respiratory System
The Senses
Sleep
Speech & Hearing
Sports Medicine
Vision
Vitamins & Minerals

THE LIFE CYCLE

Adolescence
Adulthood
Aging
Childhood
Death & Dying
The Family
Friendship & Love
Pregnancy & Birth

MEDICAL ISSUES

Careers in Health Care
Environmental Health
Folk Medicine
Health Care Delivery
Holistic Medicine
Medical Ethics
Medical Fakes & Frauds
Medical Technology
Medicine & the Law
Occupational Health
Public Health

PSYCHOLOGICAL DISORDERS AND THEIR TREATMENT

Anxiety & Phobias
Child Abuse
Compulsive Behavior
Delinquency & Criminal Behavior
Depression
Diagnosing & Treating Mental Illness
Eating Habits & Disorders
Learning Disabilities
Mental Retardation
Personality Disorders
Schizophrenia
Stress Management
Suicide

MEDICAL DISORDERS AND THEIR TREATMENT

AIDS
Allergies
Alzheimer's Disease
Arthritis
Birth Defects
Cancer
The Common Cold
Diabetes
Emergency Medicine
Gynecological Disorders
Headaches
The Hospital
Kidney Disorders
Medical Diagnosis
The Mind-Body Connection
Mononucleosis and Other Infectious Diseases
Nuclear Medicine
Organ Transplants
Pain
Physical Handicaps
Poisons & Toxins
Prescription & OTC Drugs
Sexually Transmitted Diseases
Skin Disorders
Stroke & Heart Disease
Substance Abuse
Tropical Medicine

PREVENTION AND EDUCATION: THE KEYS TO GOOD HEALTH

C. Everett Koop, M.D., Sc.D.
former Surgeon General,
U.S. Public Health Service

The issue of health education has received particular attention in recent years because of the presence of AIDS in the news. But our response to this particular tragedy points up a number of broader issues that doctors, public health officials, educators, and the public face. In particular, it points up the necessity for sound health education for citizens of all ages.

Over the past 25 years this country has been able to bring about dramatic declines in the death rates for heart disease, stroke, accidents, and for people under the age of 45, cancer. Today, Americans generally eat better and take better care of themselves than ever before. Thus, with the help of modern science and technology, they have a better chance of surviving serious—even catastrophic—illnesses. That's the good news.

But, like every phonograph record, there's a flip side, and one with special significance for young adults. According to a report issued in 1979 by Dr. Julius Richmond, my predecessor as Surgeon General, Americans aged 15 to 24 had a higher death rate in 1979 than they did 20 years earlier. The causes: violent death and injury, alcohol and drug abuse, unwanted pregnancies, and sexually transmitted diseases. Adolescents are particularly vulnerable because they are beginning to explore their own sexuality and perhaps to experiment with drugs. The need for educating young people is critical, and the price of neglect is high.

Yet even for the population as a whole, our health is still far from what it could be. Why? A 1974 Canadian government report attributed all death and disease to four broad elements: inadequacies in the health care system, behavioral factors or unhealthy life-styles, environmental hazards, and human biological factors.

To be sure, there are diseases that are still beyond the control of even our advanced medical knowledge and techniques. And despite yearnings that are as old as the human race itself, there is no "fountain of youth" to ward off aging and death. Still, there is a solution to many of the problems that undermine sound health. In a word, that solution is prevention. Prevention, which includes health promotion and education, saves lives, improves the quality of life, and in the long run, saves money.

In the United States, organized public health activities and preventive medicine have a long history. Important milestones in this country or foreign breakthroughs adopted in the United States include the improvement of sanitary procedures and the development of pasteurized milk in the late 19th century and the introduction in the mid-20th century of effective vaccines against polio, measles, German measles, mumps, and other once-rampant diseases. Internationally, organized public health efforts began on a wide-scale basis with the International Sanitary Conference of 1851, to which 12 nations sent representatives. The World Health Organization, founded in 1948, continues these efforts under the aegis of the United Nations, with particular emphasis on combating communicable diseases and the training of health care workers.

Despite these accomplishments, much remains to be done in the field of prevention. For too long, we have had a medical care system that is science- and technology-based, focused, essentially, on illness and mortality. It is now patently obvious that both the social and the economic costs of such a system are becoming insupportable.

Implementing prevention—and its corollaries, health education and promotion—is the job of several groups of people.

First, the medical and scientific professions need to continue basic scientific research, and here we are making considerable progress. But increased concern with prevention will also have a decided impact on how primary care doctors practice medicine. With a shift to health-based rather than morbidity-based medicine, the role of the "new physician" will include a healthy dose of patient education.

Second, practitioners of the social and behavioral sciences—psychologists, economists, city planners—along with lawyers, business leaders, and government officials—must solve the practical and ethical dilemmas confronting us: poverty, crime, civil rights, literacy, education, employment, housing, sanitation, environmental protection, health care delivery systems, and so forth. All of these issues affect public health.

Third is the public at large. We'll consider that very important group in a moment.

Fourth, and the linchpin in this effort, is the public health profession—doctors, epidemiologists, teachers—who must harness the professional expertise of the first two groups and the common sense and cooperation of the third, the public. They must define the problems statistically and qualitatively and then help us set priorities for finding the solutions.

To a very large extent, improving those statistics is the responsibility of every individual. So let's consider more specifically what the role of the individual should be and why health education is so important to that role. First, and most obvious, individuals can protect themselves from illness and injury and thus minimize their need for professional medical care. They can eat nutritious food; get adequate exercise; avoid tobacco, alcohol, and drugs; and take prudent steps to avoid accidents. The proverbial "apple a day keeps the doctor away" is not so far from the truth, after all.

Second, individuals should actively participate in their own medical care. They should schedule regular medical and dental checkups. Should they develop an illness or injury, they should know when to treat themselves and when to seek professional help. To gain the maximum benefit from any medical treatment that they do require, individuals must become partners in that treatment. For instance, they should understand the effects and side effects of medications. I counsel young physicians that there is no such thing as too much information when talking with patients. But the corollary is the patient must know enough about the nuts and bolts of the healing process to understand what the doctor is telling him or her. That is at least partially the patient's responsibility.

Education is equally necessary for us to understand the ethical and public policy issues in health care today. Sometimes individuals will encounter these issues in making decisions about their own treatment or that of family members. Other citizens may encounter them as jurors in medical malpractice cases. But we all become involved, indirectly, when we elect our public officials, from school board members to the president. Should surrogate parenting be legal? To what extent is drug testing desirable, legal, or necessary? Should there be public funding for family planning, hospitals, various types of medical research, and other medical care for the indigent? How should we allocate scant technological resources, such as kidney dialysis and organ transplants? What is the proper role of government in protecting the rights of patients?

What are the broad goals of public health in the United States today? In 1980, the Public Health Service issued a report aptly entitled *Promoting Health—Preventing Disease: Objectives for the Nation*. This report expressed its goals in terms of mortality and in terms of intermediate goals in education and health improvement. It identified 15 major concerns: controlling high blood pressure; improving family planning; improving pregnancy care and infant health; increasing the rate of immunization; controlling sexually transmitted diseases; controlling the presence of toxic agents and radiation in the environment; improving occupational safety and health; preventing accidents; promoting water fluoridation and dental health; controlling infectious diseases; decreasing smoking; decreasing alcohol and drug abuse; improving nutrition; promoting physical fitness and exercise; and controlling stress and violent behavior.

For healthy adolescents and young adults (ages 15 to 24), the specific goal was a 20% reduction in deaths, with a special focus on motor vehicle injuries and alcohol and drug abuse. For adults (ages 25 to 64), the aim was 25% fewer deaths, with a concentration on heart attacks, strokes, and cancers.

Smoking is perhaps the best example of how individual behavior can have a direct impact on health. Today, cigarette smoking is recognized as the single most important preventable cause of death in our society. It is responsible for more cancers and more cancer deaths than any other known agent; is a prime risk factor for heart and blood vessel disease, chronic bronchitis, and emphysema; and is a frequent cause of complications in pregnancies and of babies born prematurely, underweight, or with potentially fatal respiratory and cardiovascular problems.

Since the release of the Surgeon General's first report on smoking in 1964, the proportion of adult smokers has declined substantially, from 43% in 1965 to 30.5% in 1985. Since 1965, 37 million people have quit smoking. Although there is still much work to be done if we are to become a "smoke-free society," it is heartening to note that public health and public education efforts—such as warnings on cigarette packages and bans on broadcast advertising—have already had significant effects.

In 1835, Alexis de Tocqueville, a French visitor to America, wrote, "In America the passion for physical well-being is general." Today, as then, health and fitness are front-page items. But with the greater scientific and technological resources now available to us, we are in a far stronger position to make good health care available to everyone. And with the greater technological threats to us as we approach the 21st century, the need to do so is more urgent than ever before. Comprehensive information about basic biology, preventive medicine, medical and surgical treatments, and related ethical and public policy issues can help you arm yourself with the knowledge you need to be healthy throughout your life.

FOREWORD

Dale C. Garell, M.D.

Advances in our understanding of health and disease during the 20th century have been truly remarkable. Indeed, it could be argued that modern health care is one of the greatest accomplishments in all of human history. In the early 20th century, improvements in sanitation, water treatment, and sewage disposal reduced death rates and increased longevity. Previously untreatable illnesses can now be managed with antibiotics, immunizations, and modern surgical techniques. Discoveries in the fields of immunology, genetic diagnosis, and organ transplantation are revolutionizing the prevention and treatment of disease. Modern medicine is even making inroads against cancer and heart disease, two of the leading causes of death in the United States.

Although there is much to be proud of, medicine continues to face enormous challenges. Science has vanquished diseases such as smallpox and polio, but new killers, most notably AIDS, confront us. Moreover, we now victimize ourselves with what some have called "diseases of choice," or those brought on by drug and alcohol abuse, bad eating habits, and mismanagement of the stresses and strains of contemporary life. The very technology that is doing so much to prolong life has brought with it previously unimaginable ethical dilemmas related to issues of death and dying. The rising cost of health care is a matter of central concern to us all. And violence in the form of automobile accidents, homicide, and suicide remains the major killer of young adults.

In the past, most people were content to leave health care and medical treatment in the hands of professionals. But since the 1960s, the consumer of medical care—that is, the patient—has assumed an increasingly central role in the management of his or her own health. There has also been a new emphasis placed on prevention: People are recognizing that their own actions can help prevent many of the conditions that have caused death and disease in the past. This accounts for the growing commitment to good nutrition and regular exercise, for the increasing number of people who are choosing not to smoke, and for a new moderation in people's drinking habits.

People want to know more about themselves and their own health. They are curious about their body: its anatomy, physiology, and bio-chemistry. They want to keep up with rapidly evolving medical technologies and procedures. They are willing to educate themselves about common disorders and diseases so that they can be full partners in their own health care.

THE ENCYCLOPEDIA OF HEALTH is designed to provide the basic knowledge that readers will need if they are to take significant responsibility for their own health. It is also meant to serve as a frame of reference for further study and exploration. The encyclopedia is divided into five subsections: The Healthy Body; The Life Cycle; Medical Disorders & Their Treatment; Psychological Disorders & Their Treatment; and Medical Issues. For each topic covered by the encyclopedia, we present the essential facts about the relevant biology; the symptoms, diagnosis, and treatment of common diseases and disorders; and ways in which you can prevent or reduce the severity of health problems when that is possible. The encyclopedia also projects what may lie ahead in the way of future treatment or prevention strategies.

The broad range of topics and issues covered in the encyclopedia reflects that human health encompasses physical, psychological, social, environmental, and spiritual well-being. Just as the mind and the body are inextricably linked, so, too, is the individual an integral part of the wider world that comprises his or her family, society, and environment. To discuss health in its broadest aspect it is necessary to explore the many ways in which it is connected to such fields as law, social science, public policy, economics, and even religion. And so, the encyclopedia is meant to be a bridge between science, medical technology, the world at large, and you. I hope that it will inspire you to pursue in greater depth particular areas of interest and that you will take advantage of the suggestions for further reading and the lists of resources and organizations that can provide additional information.

CHAPTER 1

ABUSE AND ADDICTION

In this miniature painting from a 15th century Persian manuscript, a woman uses a hookah, or water pipe, to smoke hashish.

The use—and misuse—of substances that change the way a person feels are perhaps as old as humankind itself. Throughout the ages, people have sought and prized various compounds for their ability to stimulate the body, to reduce pain, to induce relaxation, to produce pleasurable intoxication, and to create a sense of spiritual transcendence.

Yet in recent decades, the abuse of such substances has become a health problem of tremendous magnitude in the United States and other nations throughout the world. The incidence of illness and death related to cigarette smoking and alcohol consumption has remained disturbingly high despite attempts to educate people about their dangers. At the same time, the illegal use of various substances continues to cause a broad spectrum of health and social problems.

The phrase *substance abuse* is now widely used to describe the improper or nonmedical use of a variety of compounds. Many of these substances, such as tobacco and alcohol, are not commonly considered "drugs," but they may nevertheless present serious threats to a person's health.

Why Do People Use Mood-Altering Substances?

In theory, any substance that can affect the way a person feels can be classified as a mood-altering substance. Such compounds are also called *psychoactive* because they act on the brain, affecting the way it perceives sensations such as exhaustion, hunger, pain, or depression. Coffee, cocaine, tobacco, marijuana, heroin, and alcohol are all considered psychoactive substances. Even food has the ability to affect the way a person feels: indulging in an ice cream sundae, for instance, may cheer a person up. For this reason, as well as the fact that eating disorders such as bulimia and anorexia nervosa share certain traits with other forms of substance abuse, experts also view food as a psychoactive substance.

Generally, people will use a mood-altering substance to do just what the term implies: to alter their mood or state of mind in a pleasurable way. Substances with mind-altering capabilities are often grouped according to their specific effects. One group, for example, includes compounds that mainly have stimulant properties—those that stimulate the central nervous system, thereby tending to offset fatigue and to make a person feel enlivened or agitated. Coffee, tea, and other caffeinated beverages; amphetamines; diet pills; tobacco (specifically its active ingredient, nicotine); cocaine; and crack cocaine are examples of substances defined by their stimulant properties. These substances are often used when a person wants to feel more awake or energetic (such as when people have a morning cup of coffee), or wants to stay awake for long periods of time. Some stimulant substances are used in the treatment of various medical and psychological disorders.

A second group of mood-altering substances is made up of compounds categorized by their depressant effects. These substances tend to depress the central nervous system, slowing down the rate at which the body operates and generally promoting relaxation and sleepiness. Beer, wine, hard liquor, heroin and other opiate drugs, sleeping pills, and tranquilizers are generally included in this group. People use these substances when they want to relax or "unwind" (as with drinking during an after-work "happy hour") or to promote sleep. These substances may also have certain medical applications.

Other mood-altering substances, such as marijuana, have actions similar to both stimulants and depressants, along with certain other properties. Hallucinogens, such as lysergic acid diethylamide (LSD) and psilocybin, are powerful psychoactive drugs that disorder the senses in a variety of ways. There is also an ever-increasing number of new pharmaceutical products and some illegally synthesized agents that have various effects on the human mind and body.

Other factors besides pleasure seeking and medication contribute to the widespread use of psychoactive substances in American society. Many people use these substances to conform with the norms of a drug-taking group. Peer pressure and the desire to be "one of the gang" may lead people to smoke, drink, or take drugs even if the effects of these substances are undesirable to them.

Furthermore, the use of certain substances can be culturally symbolic. Smoking one's first cigarette, getting drunk for the first time, or experimenting with drugs is sometimes viewed as a "rite of passage" for young people in American society—an event that signifies a movement toward adulthood. Drinking to excess is considered a sign of masculinity in many cultures. Similarly, cigarette smoking often connotes sophistication or toughness. The mass media—including films, television, and advertising—are sometimes blamed for glamorizing the use of mood-altering substances, both legal and illegal.

Alcohol abuse has been blamed on the stresses and strains of modern life, the loneliness and alienation of the city, the breakdown of the family system, and the demands of a society fixated on material success.

Escape

It is sometimes said that the stresses and strains of modern life encourage drug use. The loneliness and alienation that urban living can breed, the breakdown of the family system, boredom, and the constant demands of a society fixated on material success have all been implicated in the rise of substance abuse. Poverty, unemployment, and homelessnesss are also blamed for fostering drug use in communities where these problems exist.

The tendency of many Americans to seek ready thrills and pleasures, immediate gratification for their desires, and simple solutions to every problem is the basis for what some authorities, such as sociologist Todd Gitlin, consider a drug-taking mentality. As we will see, however, taking a drink, popping a pill, or smoking a marijuana joint in response to ordinary stress can cause much more serious problems than those it is intended to solve.

Some authorities have pointed to the quest for immediate gratification, quick thrills, and rapid solutions to problems in explaining the presence of a drug-taking mentality among large numbers of Americans.

SAY DRUG HABIT GRIPS THE NATION

United States Second Only to China in Abuse of Opium Products, Experts Affirm.

MANY PHYSICIANS VICTIMS

GREAT D.

The first st
by Mrs. Will
the use of c
and other dr
when Ernest
Coulter & Bo
torney's, had
Chief Magist
F. Lewis, Se
sociation in re
phase of the
the conferenc
night, there w

What Constitutes Abuse?

Some mood-altering substances, such as coffee and caffeinated soda, are widely available to just about anyone. Others, including cigarettes and alcohol, are legally available only to adults. Still others can be legitimately obtained only by a doctor's prescription, and some—such as cocaine, marijuana, LSD, and heroin—are illegal to use under virtually any conditions.

While some may argue that any use of an illegal substance constitutes abuse, the line separating the socially acceptable use of legal drugs from their unacceptable use is often difficult to determine. Every culture has different standards of permissible substance use, and these standards vary according to context. The social sanctions about when, where, how, and by whom a mood-altering substance may be used are often based as much on tradition as any other factor. While many restaurants offer Bloody Mary or Mimosa cocktails with a weekend brunch, most people would be taken aback if a customer ordered a glass of whiskey with his Tuesday morning breakfast. In the same way, people will accept a fellow worker who drinks eight or nine cups of coffee a day but might perceive a problem if that same person were using other types of stimulants.

Similarly, excessive or "hard" drinking may be acceptable and even encouraged among certain groups of Americans during such social events as weddings, sporting events, and concerts. In some cases, this sort of drinking may be permissible only for the men in a group and prohibited or discouraged among women.

Even the use of drugs that are illegal in some societies can be integral parts of life in other cultures. Regular use of *ganja* (marijuana) is not uncommon in certain segments of Jamaican society; daily use of *coca* (the leaf of the plant from which cocaine is derived) is common among certain cultures in Central and South America. The hallucinogen *peyote* plays a central part in the religious worship of several Native American tribes, and hallucinogenic mushrooms are commonly used among certain Indonesian cultures. On the other hand, the use of alcohol, although common in many parts of the world, is prohibited in many Islamic countries.

Clearly, many cultures use the term *abuse* to define substance use that is socially unacceptable, physically dangerous, or both. For the purposes of this book, substance abuse means any use that endangers the health and well-being of the user or those around him or her. Such endangerment can result from a single experience, as when a first-time

A trayful of illegitimate substances used for their mood-altering properties. The term substance abuse can be applied to any use of a substance—illegitimate or not—that endangers the health and well-being of both the user and persons in the user's surroundings.

cocaine user suffers a heart attack, or from more sustained use, such as when a moderate drinker causes an accident by driving while intoxicated. But the concept of substance abuse is generally tied to the concept of *addiction*—a compulsion to use a drug or substance that is beyond the user's control.

What Is Addiction?

The term *addiction* generally indicates a state that involves one of two sorts of substance (or drug) dependence. *Psychological dependence* is characterized by an overwhelming desire to repeat the use of a particular drug to produce pleasure or avoid discomfort. It can be extremely powerful, producing intense craving for a substance as well as its compulsive use. *Physical dependence* occurs when the body adapts chemically to a drug. This type of dependence is characterized by the development of *tolerance* to the drug's effects and by a syndrome of withdrawal upon ceasing to use the drug. Because psychological dependence on a substance has often been shown to involve biological changes in brain chemistry, some researchers maintain that it is incorrect to speak of a purely psychological addiction.

A person is said to have developed a tolerance to a drug when the amount taken needs to be continually increased to achieve the same effects that were once produced by smaller amounts. A withdrawal syndrome (also known as an abstinence syndrome) occurs when a person experiences any number of unpleasant—and often dangerous—physical symptoms upon abruptly stopping the use of a drug. These symptoms can vary according to the drug and the amount used and may include severe muscle cramps, nausea, insomnia, convulsions, delirium, and hallucinations, and in certain cases can lead to death.

The "Biopsychosocial" Model of Addiction

Whatever the substance or type of dependence, many factors contribute to the addictive state. During the 1980s it became common for research scientists to use a biopsychosocial model to evaluate addiction and addictive behavior. This approach assumes that any addiction is the result of certain biological, psychological, and sociological or environmental factors that interact with one another.

One biological theory for explaining addiction is the theory of *genetic predisposition*. Its proponents maintain that certain addictive traits are hereditary; that is, they can be passed on from parent to child. Accordingly, the son of alcoholic parents would be more likely to become an alcoholic himself than would the son of nonalcoholic parents. Another possible biological factor in any genetic predisposition to addiction may be a shortage of certain natural chemicals in the body, such as endorphins, a group of substances that help regulate mood and emotion. Researchers believe that such drugs as heroin mimic the actions of endorphins, and that addiction may therefore partly result from an effort by the body to correct shortages of endorphins and other chemical imbalances through the use of heroin and other drugs (see chapter 6).

Psychological factors that may increase a tendency toward addictive behavior are certain personality traits, such as low self-esteem, frequent depression, passivity, the inability to relax or to defer gratification, and the inability to communicate effectively. Another psychological factor in addiction is the expectation that frequent substance users develop about the effects of the substance they use. The more often a substance succeeds in producing the expected or desired effect, such as relaxation, the more likely a person will be to return to that particular substance, even if the effect could just as well be achieved by other, more wholesome means, such as reading a book or riding a bicycle.

In addition to these mechanisms, many social and environmental factors are believed to encourage addictive behavior. Modeling, represented by drug and alcohol use by peers and parents, can play a role in a person's addiction to such substances, as can direct or indirect pressure from peers and the sharing of common values or beliefs about the benefits of mood-altering substances. Lack of intimate relationships with one's family or friends, along with the absence of rewarding, productive work, also seem to be connected with addictive tendencies. Research on heroin addiction among soldiers in the Vietnam War has supported the belief that high-stress environments may increase the

Social drinking is a widely accepted behavior pattern in modern society, but it can become a psychological cover for serious alcohol abuse.

rate of addiction among those who must cope with them. The pressures of living in lower-income, inner-city environments have similarly been tied to higher levels of addictive behavior.

An example of the way three sets of factors—biological, psychological, and social—interact with each other might involve a person who has a tendency toward depression that is reinforced if she is living or working in an unpleasant, high-stress environment. If this person is also the child of an alcoholic, then an occasional drink, taken to relieve stress, may be the start of a tailspin into addictive behavior.

Is Addiction a Disease?

Addiction, especially when it involves illegal substances, is a widely misunderstood and emotionally charged issue. Many people condemn the addict as a criminal or deviant for having "chosen" to abuse a particular substance. The fact that some addicts are driven to crime to support their habits strengthens this impression.

Although the academic debate continues about whether or not addiction should be defined as a disease, many treatment professionals consider it one. According to Dr. Arnold Washton, director of a New York City drug-abuse treatment center and widely published expert on addictive disorders, defining addiction as a disease can help the patient through the recovery process by removing the guilt associated with his or her addictive behavior and emphasizing the need to treat all mood-altering drugs and drug-related habits as sources of disease.

Furthermore, addiction fits many of the criteria used to define other diseases: it can be diagnosed from certain signs and symptoms; it is generally a progressive disorder that if ignored grows worse with the passage of time, and it can be treated through various techniques, as discussed in chapter 7.

Combating the Problem

According to 1990 estimates by the U.S. Department of Health and Human Services (HHS), more than 1,000 Americans die every day as a result of illnesses related to tobacco smoking. More than 500 persons die every day from alcohol-related accidents and diseases, and 20 die each day from other types of drug overdoses and drug-related homicides. In the early 1980s, before the rise of crack cocaine and its violent subculture, estimates from some cities indicated that 25% of all homicides were related to illegal drug trafficking. The HHS estimated that the overall national cost of alcohol and drug abuse for 1988—in terms of medical treatment, lost productivity, and law enforcement—was approximately $144 billion.

Combating the problem of substance abuse can be an expensive endeavor. The U.S. Government spent an estimated $6.5 billion on law enforcement and criminal justice related to illegal substances in 1990 alone. And yet, with courts overcrowded by drug-law violators and prisons similarly bursting at the seams, it appears that either more money or a change in strategy will still be needed to capture and prosecute all of those involved in marketing illicit substances.

Rather than treating the so-called drug problem as a criminal matter, some people assert that it should be addressed as an issue of public health. This approach, however, depends on the availability of effective treatment facilities for substance abusers. Treatment takes a number of forms, ranging from drop-in counseling and self-help groups (such as Alcoholics Anonymous or similar "12-step" organizations) to hospital detoxification programs and "therapeutic communities" that provide a group-home setting for recovering addicts (see chapter 7).

The trouble with such treatment programs at present is that too few of them exist. Those that are available, especially in those areas where substance abuse is widespread, have long waiting lists. Weeks or even months pass before addicts can be accommodated. As a result, many addicts are discouraged from even applying for treatment.

Even under ideal conditions, rehabilitation after substance abuse is not always successful. Drug and alcohol addiction are commonly viewed as chronic conditions. Addicts are always capable of a release—that is, a return to addictive patterns of behavior. Therefore, educating people about the dangers of drug and alcohol abuse has become another important strategy in dealing with the drug problem and is part of what is now referred to as substance abuse prevention.

Preventing drug and alcohol abuse entails more than communicating facts about these problems; it also involves teaching interpersonal skills that will enable a person to resist peer and societal pressure to experiment with mood-altering substances. Although prevention efforts may be targeted at any age group, most are aimed at young people between the ages of 13 and 18.

While efforts at preventing substance abuse are usually conducted by schools and community groups, the media—which has often been criticized for promoting substance abuse through tobacco and alcohol advertising—has addressed this problem in recent years with growing numbers of television documentaries, news specials, and dramas, as well as motion pictures. During the 1980s, a coalition of advertisers, broadcasters, and film producers joined together to form the Partnership for a Drug-Free America—an organization whose objective was to "de-normalize" illegal drug use in America using the techniques of commercial advertising. The group produced more than 250 antidrug messages for print, radio, and television between 1987 and 1990, and research indicates that its work has been effective in changing attitudes toward drugs.

Related Issues

The effects of substance abuse reach beyond the abusers themselves. Drug- and alcohol-impaired pregnancies are responsible for a disturbing number of premature births and birth defects. In particular, the use of crack cocaine by young mothers has been noted with increasing frequency; 1989 estimates by the U.S. government put the number of *cocaine babies* born annually at 100,000. Other estimates indicate that as many as 375,000 infants annually are exposed to illicit drugs while still in the womb.

Alcohol use by expectant mothers has also been recognized as a serious problem. Fetal alcohol syndrome (FAS) is a severe disorder appearing in infants whose mothers are known to have drunk heavily during their pregnancies. FAS can result in a wide range of permanent physical and mental deficiencies that often require long-term care and treatment. The U.S. Department of Health and Human Services estimated that $1.6 billion was spent on these services in 1985.

Also associated with substance abuse is acquired immune deficiency syndrome (AIDS), first identified in intravenous (or IV) drug abusers in 1981. Because of the way the AIDS virus is spread—through the exchange of body fluids with an infected person—the practice of sharing hypodermic needles has led to rapid spread of the disease among IV drug users. Because AIDS can also be transmitted by sexual contact and from a mother to her unborn child, the children and sexual partners of IV drug users are also at high risk for getting the disease.

Clearly, substance abuse is a multifaceted problem that will not be resolved by simple, single-minded tactics. It affects not only the abusers and their families and friends but also society as a whole, through the automobile and industrial accidents caused by persons under the influence of mood-altering substances, the higher crime rates connected with drug and alcohol abuse, and rising health care costs.

CHAPTER 2

ABUSE OF COMMON SUBSTANCES

This 19th-century illustration of game-sters caricatures both the setting in which tobacco was likely to be smoked and the unsavory character of those who practiced this habit.

Although substance abuse is commonly associated with such illicit drugs as cocaine and heroin, the abuse of legally available substances is much more widespread. Cigarettes, alcoholic beverages, and coffee—none of which is generally considered a "drug"—are all mood-altering substances subject to abuse, with effects on the body that often bear striking similarity to those of many illicit drugs.

Tobacco

Tobacco is the common name for the dried leaves of the tobacco plant, *Nicotiana tabacum*, a member of the nightshade family of plants, which contain various substances that affect the nervous system. Tobacco is a leafy, fast-growing annual plant that is cultivated in various parts of the world. The United States and China are the two leading producers of tobacco.

Today, the use of tobacco is commonplace and accepted in most parts of the world. This, however, was not always the case. In the past, political and religious leaders in many countries have viewed its use with disdain, and at various times and in various places, smoking in public has been considered a criminal offense. In both Turkey and Germany, it was once punishable by death.

Although tobacco was known to natives of the Western Hemisphere as early as A.D. 100, Europeans did not encounter the plant until Christopher Columbus observed its use in the West Indies in 1492. Natives of the Caribbean Islands used tobacco both for smoking and as a snuff, a preparation that is inhaled into the nostrils. The small tube through which snuff was inhaled was known alternately as a "tobago" or "tobaca," which is the source of the plant's modern name.

As smoking and the use of snuff became popular throughout other parts of the world during the 16th and 17th centuries, cultivation of the tobacco plant became a profitable enterprise. The new settlers in North America, particularly those in the colony of Virginia, began what would eventually become the United States's multibillion-dollar tobacco industry. With the introduction of the cigarette in the 1850s, tobacco use became even more widespread. In 1990, an estimated 53 million Americans—nearly 27% of the population aged 12 and older—were regular cigarette smokers, according to a survey by the U.S. National Institute of Drug Abuse (NIDA).

Tobacco smoke is known to contain some 4,000 different compounds. Among its major psychoactive components are acetaldehyde, a chemical with sedative properties, and nicotine, a stimulant. Consequently, users may claim that tobacco smoking helps them both to relax and to remain alert and focused on a particular task.

Among the many celebrities who have succumbed to diseases caused by tobacco smoking is actor Humphrey Bogart, a victim of lung cancer.

Research has shown that nicotine in particular can produce marked psychological and physical dependence. One of its effects seems to be tolerance, with users tending to smoke increasing numbers of cigarettes to achieve the same effects. When they stop smoking, heavy smokers also often experience withdrawal symptoms, including a decrease in heart rate and blood pressure, insomnia (inability to sleep), headache, fatigue, nervousness, and tremors. The health risks of cigarette smoking have been clearly documented. Smoking was first linked to lung cancer as far back as 1936 and is now believed to contribute to other diseases, including heart disease, emphysema, bronchitis, and pneumonia. In addition to lung cancer, smokers have a higher incidence of cancer of the mouth, larynx, esophagus, pancreas, and urinary tract than do nonsmokers.

The *Journal of the American Medical Association* notes that current estimates of the annual number of smoking-related deaths in the United States range from 270,000 to 485,000. Excluding deaths resulting from drug- or alcohol-related auto accidents or homicides, tobacco use kills more than twice as many Americans as alcohol, legal drugs, and illegal substances combined.

Quitting smoking can be extremely difficult, but millions have succeeded. Many ex-smokers have managed to conquer nicotine addiction on their own. For others, various methods of treating the addiction can help them to give up the smoking habit. Some of these methods involve the use of chewing gum or nasal sprays that contain nicotine or other drugs, such as clonidine, that can reduce the addict's craving for nicotine. Other methods focus on improving exercise and dietary habits.

Besides the tens of millions of Americans who smoke, approximately 7 million others regularly use smokeless tobacco, in the form of snuff or chewing tobacco, according to NIDA statistics. This habit has been linked to oral cancer and can produce nicotine dependence in the same way as cigarette smoking.

Caffeine

Caffeine is a naturally occurring chemical compound found in certain plants. It acts as a stimulant of the central nervous system, increasing an individual's state of alertness, interfering with sleep, and sup-

Chewing tobacco can cause as much harm as smoking it. Sean Marsee, an award-winning high school athlete of Ada, Oklahoma, was in outstanding physical health until he began chewing tobacco at age 18. Only slightly more than a year later, he died of oral cancer caused by his chewing habit.

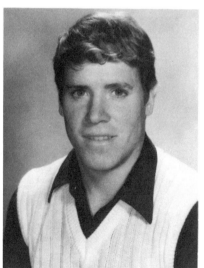

pressing appetite. Such beverages as coffee, tea, cocoa, and various sodas and soft drinks (especially colas) may contain caffeine. Caffeine is also sold in a variety of over-the-counter drugs designed either to combat fatigue or to reduce the appetite. It is sometimes used as an ingredient in cough medicines and cold remedies. The seeds of the cola, cacao, (from which chocolate is produced), and coffee plants, along with the leaves of *Thea sinensis* (the plant from which common tea is produced), all contain caffeine. These items have been used for thousands of years in various parts of the world for their stimulant effects. In the United States today, it is unusual to find anyone other than infants who does not consume caffeine in one way or another.

Although it appears to be fairly safe when used in moderation, caffeine has been shown to be both physically and psychologically addictive. Withdrawal symptoms, including headache and fatigue, have been demonstrated when persons who regularly drink four cups of coffee a day (approximately 400 milligrams of caffeine) switch to decaffeinated coffee.

Overuse of caffeine will generally result in feelings of overstimulation and jitteriness, often referred to as "coffee nerves." Some research has linked high levels of caffeine consumption to incidents of pancreatic cancer and heart trouble, but the evidence on this appears inconclusive.

On the other hand, concern has recently increased about heavy caffeine intake by pregnant mothers. Studies have indicated that large quantities of caffeine may retard the growth of the unborn child and increase the possibility of other complications of pregnancy. Although these studies are not conclusive, some physicians recommend that women who are heavy caffeine users either eliminate caffeine from their diet during pregnancy or at least limit their intake of it.

Alcohol

According to the 1990 NIDA Household Survey on Drug Abuse, nearly 103 million Americans, or 51% of the population, had used alcohol in some form in the month prior to the survey. That figure includes five million persons between the ages of 12 and 17. Of all the drugs mentioned in the survey (tobacco was included; caffeine and medicine used under a physician's care were not), alcohol was the most widely used.

Alcohol is produced mainly by fermentation, a process that occurs when microscopic yeast organisms transform the natural sugars in fruits and grains into ethyl alcohol. Both beer and wine are produced in this way. The process of distillation, used to make whiskey and other so-called hard liquors, involves heating fermented liquids to obtain a product with a higher alcohol content than can be obtained by fermentation alone.

Like opiates and barbiturates, alcohol acts as a central nervous system depressant, reducing the activity of a number of functions governed by the brain. Depending on how much is taken, it may help bring about relaxation or induce sleep and in larger doses may act as an anesthetic or painkilling agent. Alcohol often acts to reduce inhibitions, releasing behavior that an individual might not ordinarily exhibit. In moderate doses (one or two drinks), alcohol can make the average adult drinker feel a sense of relaxation and increased self-confidence.

By inhibiting the region of the brain that controls heart rate and the rate of breathing, alcohol initially produces an increase in both of these functions, which is why some people feel stimulated upon having their first drink. Alcohol also causes blood vessels near the surface of the skin to dilate, or open up, which is why some people who have been drinking will appear red in the face. This effect has given rise to the myth that drinking alcohol will keep one warm in cold weather. The truth is that while it may at first create a warming sensation from blood rushing to the skin and extremities, the body will ultimately lose heat more rapidly than if alcohol had not been consumed.

Historical records indicate that alcohol is the oldest drug known to man. A form of wine known as mead is believed to have been used as far back as 8000 B.C. Later, ancient Egyptian, Greek, and Roman mythology often referred to the use of fermented alcohol (Dionysus and Bacchus, were the Greek and Roman gods of wine, respectively). Between A.D. 1000 and 1250, the distillation process allowed the widespread production of stronger alcoholic beverages in Europe, though these were most often used by the upper classes as medicines.

The problem of excessive drunkenness was often mentioned in the work of such 16th-century English writers as William Shakespeare and Thomas Nash. To address the issue in England, Parliament found it necessary to pass the Act to Repress the Odious and Loathsome Sin of Drunkenness in 1606, the first extensive effort to legislate moderation of alcohol use. England's alcohol problem continued, however, and grew with the introduction of distilled liquor—in the form of "geneva," or gin—from Holland in the mid-17th century. Between the early and mid-18th century, government concern over excessive gin drinking among the poor led to many unsuccessful attempts at discouraging its use. But the large profits earned from the sale and taxation of gin, combined with the attractiveness of its low cost to the country's poor, made its prohibition impractical.

During the colonial period in America, alcohol use was common even among the Puritans. It was not perceived to be a major problem until distilled liquor became the predominant alcoholic beverage in the period following the Revolutionary War. As in England, efforts to discourage the use of alcohol, including both high rates of taxation and legal restrictions, were largely unsuccessful.

The era of *Prohibition* in the United States, which lasted from 1920 to 1933, grew out of 19th-century efforts to eliminate the use of alcohol in America, often referred to as the *temperance movement*. While state laws prohibiting the use and sale of alcohol have been enacted at various times in American history, the passage of the 18th Amendment to the U.S. Constitution on January 16, 1920, marked the first and only time a national law was passed outlawing the sale of alcohol.

Prohibition proved unsuccessful for a number of reasons, including the difficulty of enforcing it. Hundreds of thousands of illegal distillery operations and speakeasies—private clubs serving illegal or boot-legged liquor—were set up across the country, and many Americans simply ignored the 18th Amendment in order to continue using alcohol. Another unforeseen result of prohibition was the death rate from people drinking contaminated liquor. By 1929, millions of Americans had died from consuming impure alcohol. Prohibition was finally repealed in 1933 with the passage of the 21st Amendment. With the exception of certain communities, commonly known as dry towns, alcohol can today be legally sold, purchased, and consumed by adults throughout the United States. By contrast, its use remains illegal in many other countries, notably those in which a majority of citizens practice Islam—a religion that prohibits the consumption of alcohol.

Although alcohol is legal in the United States, it has a high potential for abuse and presents definite health risks. Probably the most common ailment among alcohol users is the hangover, which is often experienced the morning after a night of excessive drinking. A hangover is characterized by headache, nausea, dryness of the mouth and throat, and occasionally tremors.

Although hangovers are temporary, they may in some cases indicate symptoms of mild alcohol withdrawal and the beginning of an alcohol dependence. Severe alcohol withdrawal, known as delirium tremens (or DTs), can be fatal; it involves anxiety, hallucinations, delirium, sweating, sleeplessness, and sometimes seizures and generally lasts from 1 to 10 days, depending on the severity of the addiction.

A Contract for Life
Between Parent and Teenager
The SADD Drinking-Driver Contract

Besides harming the user directly through such diseases as cirrhosis of the liver, alcoholic beverages are responsible for tens of thousands of automobile-related deaths each year, many of them among young persons. The written contract shown here obligates a teenager who has been drinking not to drive, but instead to call his or her parent for transportation at any hour and under any circumstances, and binds the parent to provide that transportation.

Drinking and smoking during pregnancy can impair the health of both the unborn infant and its mother. For the infant, the effects of its mother's drinking can include birth defects and the condition known as fetal alcohol syndrome, *which reduces the infant's birth weight and growth rate.*

Heavy and persistent use of alcohol can seriously damage various parts of the body. One of these is the liver, the impaired function of which can lead to cirrhosis (scarring) of the liver and alcoholic hepatitis, among other diseases. Pancreatitis, an inflammation of the pancreas, and diseases of the stomach, including gastritis and bleeding ulcers, have also been attributed to heavy drinking, as have a wide variety of other ailments, including heart disease, various forms of cancer, brain damage, nerve disorders, and malnutrition.

In addition to causing disease, alcohol abuse is responsible for many accidents. In 1989, an estimated 17,849 Americans were killed in alcohol-related motor vehicle crashes, according to the Federal Centers for Disease Control. While this figure represents a 12% decrease from the 20,356 persons killed in 1982—part of a steady decrease in such deaths throughout the 1980s—alcohol is still thought to play a part in at least 40% of all traffic deaths.

The use of alcohol by pregnant women can subject their infants to fetal alcohol syndrome. Infants suffering from this syndrome may have low birth weight and slower growth rate than normal infants. They may also be afflicted with facial deformations. Mild to moderate retardation, learning disabilities, and emotional disorders are other common effects of fetal alcohol syndrome.

Alcohol addiction, otherwise known as alcoholism, is a chronic problem in both the United States and many other countries around the world. Approximately one in ten users of alcohol will be affected with alcoholism. Persons with alcoholism typically experience a physical dependence that is characterized by severe withdrawal symptoms, and they become tolerant to the effects of alcohol.

As with other addictions, the causes of alcoholism are variously explained in terms of biological, psychological, and social factors (see chapter 1). Research has shown, however, that biological factors are especially relevant. Experts estimate that as many as one in four children born to alcoholic parents will themselves eventually become alcoholic.

Treating Alcoholism

Like other addictions, alcoholism is treatable. Treatment for alcoholism takes many forms. One of the most common involves changing the drinker's attitude toward and behavior with alcohol. Deeply committed to this task is *Alcoholics Anonymous* (AA), a network of self-help

Many institutions now provide treatment programs for alcohol and drug addiction. Such programs have rehabilitated thousands of persons from addiction, among them former First Lady Betty Ford, shown here.

groups made up exclusively of recovering alcoholics who seek support in kicking their habit and remaining sober once they have quit. Begun in the 1930s, AA now has groups around the world. Many towns have more than one local chapter, and the organization's self-help philosophy has given rise to numerous spin-off groups. Other forms of treating alcoholism involve psychotherapeutic techniques and certain drugs that can limit a craving for liquor (such as emetine, which induces vomiting when a person using it also drinks alcohol). While the success rates of treatment for alcohol addiction vary, many people have overcome their dependency. (For a more detailed discussion of alcohol treatment, see chapter 7.)

As in the case of cigarette smoking, many young people have come to perceive the use of alcohol as a rite of passage—an activity that marks the transition from childhood to adulthood. Though it qualifies as a legal drug, various public and private groups have worked to reduce access to alcohol by minors. Many states have increased the minimum drinking age from 18 to 21 years, and various private, public, and governmental organizations have taken action over the years to limit the advertising of alcoholic beverages on radio, television, and in newspapers and magazines.

Inhalants

Many common household chemicals—among them cleaning fluids, gasoline, model glue, aerosol sprays (including spray paints), lacquer, paint thinner, and nail polish remover—give off fumes that can produce a short-lived euphoria when inhaled. Ether and amyl nitrate, two substances with legitimate medical applications, have similar properties, as does nitrous oxide, a gas used by dentists as an anesthetic agent and by manufacturers as a propellant in canned whipped cream.

When used as intoxicants, these substances are known collectively as *inhalants*, in reference to the way they are generally abused. According to the 1990 NIDA Household Survey, over 10 million Americans have used inhalants for the purpose of intoxication at least once in their lives, and more than 1.1 million had used them at least once in the month previous to the NIDA survey. Those between the ages of 12 and

25 make up the vast majority of recent users. In general, the use of inhalants seems to be limited to experimentation by teenagers and young adults, but may pose real health risks, though more research is needed to determine its long-term effects.

Inhalants are popularly abused substances because they are cheap, legal, and easy to obtain. Although their immediate effect may be to stimulate the user, inhalants act mainly as central nervous system depressants, causing symptoms such as dizziness, confusion, slurred speech, and drowsiness. Hallucinations and delusions are also common, and nausea and vomiting may occur as well. The euphoric state begins almost immediately after inhalation and will last anywhere from several minutes to an hour, depending on the amount and nature of the inhalant used.

Inhalants such as glue, gasoline, and other liquid chemicals are generally consumed by emptying the substance into a container or paper bag or onto a rag. The fumes from the substance are then inhaled deeply. Nitrous oxide may be inhaled directly from large tanks (such as those used by dentists for anesthesia) or from pressurized whipped-cream cans. Small cartridges of nitrous oxide gas, sold primarily for use with commercial whipped cream dispensers and referred to as *whippets*, are inhaled either from a dispenser or by releasing the cartridge's contents into a balloon.

Inhalants can cause numerous health problems, which vary from one substance to another. Thus, inhaling gasoline fumes can cause lead poisoning, while inhaling carbon tetrachloride (a cleaning solution often used as an inhalant) may cause liver damage, kidney failure, or both. Brain damage has been noted in many chronic inhalant users, and deaths have been reported from heart or lung failure caused by inhalant abuse.

Partial tolerance to an inhalant may develop with its frequent use, and psychological dependence may also occur. There is no evidence, however, that inhalants produce withdrawal symptoms.

CHAPTER 3

PRESCRIPTION DRUGS

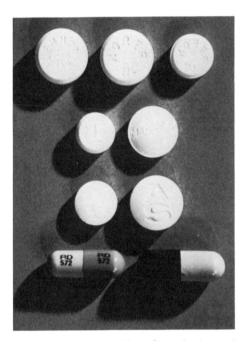

Methaqualone, sold as Quaalude and other brand names, is one of many drugs that were widely abused during the 1970s. It has been removed from the legitimate drug market.

Like alcohol and tobacco, many other mood-altering substances with a high potential for abuse can nevertheless be obtained and used legally. The medical profession considers such psychoactive drugs as barbiturates, amphetamines, and tranquilizers useful for treating certain disorders and commonly prescribes them throughout the world.

The abuse of these types of drugs, however, constitutes a substantial health problem. According to 1990 NIDA statistics, more than 24 million Americans over the age of 12 reported using psychoactive prescription drugs, either without a prescription or in a way other than that advised by their doctor, at least once in their lifetime. Furthermore, the misuse of these types of drugs leads to thousands of visits to hospital emergency rooms each year, according to reports from the NIDA Drug Abuse Warning Network (DAWN).

Sedatives

Sedative drugs, also referred to as sedative hypnotics or sleeping pills, are prescribed by physicians to treat severe anxiety and sleeplessness, as well as epilepsy. They are also used as anesthetic agents in surgery. The various types of barbiturates are perhaps the most commonly used sedatives; other drugs, such as flurazepam (brand name Dalmane), ethchlorvynol (brand name Placidyl), and glutethimide (brand name Doriden) are similar in action to barbiturates. Methaqualone (also known as Quaalude) is a sedative drug that acquired a widespread reputation for abuse during the 1970s but has since been taken off the legitimate drug market. Barbiturates and similar sedatives are usually taken orally in the form of capsules or tablets.

Sedative drugs act to depress the central nervous system. Although they are known to affect the cortex of the brain—which is responsible for sensation throughout the body, as well as voluntary movement and a host of other high-level functions—the heart, and the respiratory system, the exact way in which sedatives work is unknown. In moderate doses, sedative drugs can reduce feelings of anxiety, creating a state of euphoria and sometimes excitation; they will also cause drowsiness and sedation. Sedative intoxication is similar to alcohol intoxication and is characterized by slurred speech, impaired coordination, and confusion.

The chemist Adolph von Baeyer synthesized the first barbiturate drug in Germany in 1863. By the early 1900s, a variety of barbiturates were in wide use in the United States and elsewhere as sleep-inducing agents, replacing compounds such as alcohol and opiates. The initial enthusiasm for these drugs waned with reports of their extensive abuse during the mid-20th century, and by the 1980s other drugs had been

The German chemist Adolph von Baeyer, who synthesized barbituric acid, the first barbiturate, in 1863.

developed that took the place of barbiturates and barbiturate-type drugs for treating anxiety and promoting sleep.

The more than 2,000 different types of barbiturates are generally divided into categories according to their mode of action. Phenobarbital is the most common of the long-acting barbiturates; its effects generally last between six and eight hours. Short-acting barbiturates, which may last from two to six hours, include pentobarbital (brand name Nembutal), secobarbital (brand name Seconal) and amobarbital (brand name Amytal). Secobarbital and amobarbital are often marketed in combination under the brand name Tuinal. Finally, there are ultra-short-acting barbiturates such as sodium pentothal, which are used to produce rapid sedation; their effects last only an hour or less. In general, it is the short-duration, fast-acting barbiturates mentioned above that are most widely abused.

Barbiturates and other similar sedatives are highly addictive. They can produce severe physical and psychological dependence, and tolerance to their effects will also develop with continued use. The rapidity with which psychological dependence on the barbiturates can develop—sometimes within as little as three weeks—is one reason why doctors have come to favor tranquilizers over barbiturates and barbiturate-type sedatives for treating stress and sleeping disorders.

Withdrawal from barbiturates can be life-threatening. The severity of the withdrawal depends on how much of the drug has been taken and for how long. Abruptly stopping the use of a barbiturate after it has been taken in large doses over the course of a month or more can result in severe convulsions, delirium, and hallucinations similar to the delirium tremens that occurs in alcohol withdrawal. Other symptoms of barbiturate withdrawal include anxiety, insomnia, nausea, and vomiting. Withdrawal generally begins between 12 and 24 hours after the last administration of a barbiturate and increases to maximum severity after five to seven days; it may continue for as long as two weeks. Full recovery from barbiturate withdrawal usually takes at least a month.

During the mid-1980s, barbiturates were responsible for as many as 75% of all drug-related deaths, mainly as a result of overdose. This high death rate can be attributed to two specific characteristics of barbiturates. One is that while tolerance to a barbiturate will develop with its continued use, this tolerance does not dramatically change the amount of the drug that constitutes an overdose. Thus, the difference between an intoxicating dose and a lethal dose of a barbiturate becomes smaller as the user increases the dosage in order to overcome tolerance. The other factor that contributes to the death rate from barbiturate use is the way barbiturates interact with alcohol. Because both of these substances are metabolized, or broken down inside the body, by the liver, they sharply reduce the effectiveness of this vital organ when taken in combination with one another. As a result, both substances reach greater concentrations in the body and remain in the body for longer periods before they are broken down. This increases their effects and also increases the possibility of an overdose.

Because withdrawal from barbiturates and similar sedatives is so severe, treatment for abuse of these drugs generally involves a period of controlled *detoxification* within a hospital or other medical institution, during which the patient's dosage is slowly decreased. Following this, treatment may take place in a group resembling Alcoholics Anonymous or through some other program for behavior modification.

Tranquilizers

Until the 1950s, the drug most commonly used for reducing stress and combating anxiety was alcohol. Barbiturate sedatives were also used but presented various problems, including those discussed above. Clearly there would be a market for a drug that would help people cope with the moderate stress of everyday life.

The first such tranquilizer, meprobamate (brand name Miltown), was introduced in the United States in 1951 and was widely recognized for its anxiety-reducing properties. During the 1960s, a group of tranquilizing drugs known collectively as benzodiazepines were developed and were also found to be extremely effective for controlling stress, along with other applications. Among the drugs in this family are chlordiazepoxide (brand name Librium), diazepam (brand name Valium), alprazolam (brand name Xanax), and lorazepam (brand name Ativan).

Like many drugs through the ages, tranquilizers were at first perceived as being all-purpose "miracle drugs." They were widely prescribed for all sorts of common ailments, including nervousness, stress, muscle tension, and mild insomnia. For many years, in fact, Valium was the most commonly prescribed drug in the United States.

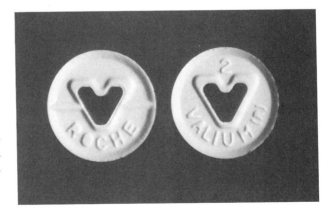

Tablets of Valium, the brand name for the tranquilizer diazepam. A member of the family of tranquilizers known as benzodiazepines, Valium has proven highly effective in the treatment of psychological stress and anxiety but has also been widely abused.

However, it soon became clear that tranquilizers were as suscep-tible to abuse as other mood-altering drugs, and perhaps more so. Drugs of this sort were commonly prescribed for daily use over long periods of time, and psychological dependence on them was common. During the 1980s it was estimated that as many as 1.5 million Americans were addicted to some form of benzodiazepine tranquilizers. In addition, a more general misuse of tranquilizers—often involving use without a prescription or in ways other than those prescribed—became common and remains so. The 1990 NIDA Household Survey estimated that nearly 8.6 million persons age 12 and older had misused tranquilizers at least once and that over a million had misused them during the month prior to the survey. Overall, it is estimated that Americans consume more than 3.5 billion tranquilizers each year.

In addition to psychological addiction, tranquilizers can induce physical dependence. Such dependence generally occurs with the regular use of these drugs over a period of more than three months, although it can also develop after only four to six weeks of use. Withdrawal from tranquilizers may produce varying degrees of anxiety and insomnia; more severe cases can resemble barbiturate withdrawal and are characterized by convulsions and delirium. Symptoms of withdrawal may not develop for seven to ten days after the last dose, which can lead a frequent user to believe that he or she has bypassed the problem of withdrawal. For this reason, tranquilizers should never be discontinued without consulting a physician.

Antipsychotics and Antidepressants

Drugs such as chlorpromazine (brand name Thorazine), haloperidol (brand name Haldol), and thioridazine (brand name Mellaril) are generally known as antipsychotics, or "major tranquilizers." These drugs are used most often for treating patients suffering from severe mental disorders. While antipsychotics do behave as central nervous system depressants, the exact way in which they work is unknown.

Although abuse and misuse of the antipsychotic drugs is uncom-mon, it does occur. These drugs can be particularly dangerous when taken in combination with alcohol or other depressant drugs such as opiates or sedatives.

Because they do not appear to produce either dependence or tolerance, the antipsychotic drugs are not considered addictive. However, abuse of these drugs can be fatal, and their continual use has been shown to produce a disorder known as *tardive dyskensia*, a potentially permanent syndrome that consists of involuntary twitching and muscle spasms.

The antidepressant drugs include amitriptyline (brand name Elavil), imipramine (brand name Tofranil), and doxepin (brand name Sinequan). As their name implies, they are used either alone or in combination with certain tranquilizers to treat severe depression. They do not produce physical addiction but may give rise to a mild psychological dependence. As with the antipsychotic drugs, the use of antidepressants in combination with other drugs—particularly alcohol and other sedatives—is dangerous.

The use of one new antidepressant drug, fluoxetine (brand name Prozac)—first introduced in December 1987—was responsible for a great many emergency room episodes and deaths between the beginning of 1988 and the end of 1989, according to DAWN reports.

Stimulants

The drugs known as *stimulants* promote wakefulness, increase alertness, and accelerate various physical functions such as the heartbeat and breathing. The best-known stimulant drugs belong to the group of substances called *amphetamines*, which includes amphetamine sulfate (brand name Benzedrine), dextroamphetamine sulfate (brand name Dexedrine), and methamphetamine hydrochloride (brand name Desoxyn). Various combinations of amphetamine and dextroamphetamine are marketed under the brand names Biphetamine and Obetrol.

Also known as speed, amphetamines have two main effects. One is the relief of fatigue, with an increased feeling of alertness and endurance, accompanied by an increase in the breathing rate and blood pressure. The other is to decrease the appetite, a characteristic that

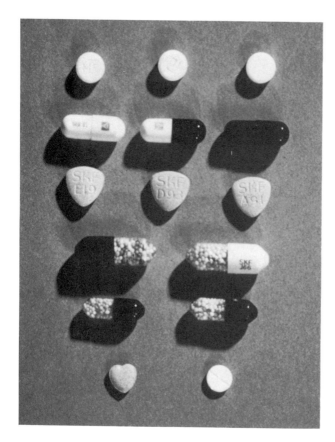

A variety of commercially available amphetamine drugs such as those shown here, as well as others made illegally, are used for their stimulant and appetite-suppressing properties. Abuse of these drugs can lead to irritability, anxiety, depression, and psychosis.

has led physicians to prescribe amphetamines for the treatment of obesity and overeating disorders. Amphetamine-like stimulants such as phenmetrazine hydrochloride (brand name Preludin) and phentermine hydrochloride (brand name Fastin) are also prescribed for weight loss.

In addition, amphetamines are prescribed to treat narcolepsy, a relatively rare disorder in which unseen or seemingly minor events may trigger the onset of sleep. Because their stimulant properties have the paradoxical effect of quieting restless behavior, amphetamines are also commonly used for treating hyperactivity (also known as hyperkinesis or attention deficit disorder) in children. The amphetamines accomplish this by increasing the hyperactive child's ability to concentrate. Pemoline (brand name Cylert) and methylphenidate hydrochloride (brand name Ritalin) are nonamphetamine stimulants used for treating children with short attention spans.

Amphetamines are used in a variety of forms. Those prescribed by a physician are most often dispensed in the form of tablets and capsules intended for oral use. However, abusers will often empty amphetamine capsules or grind the tablets to obtain a fine powder, which can then be either inhaled into the nostrils or mixed with water and injected into a vein by using a hypodermic needle.

Illicitly manufactured amphetamines generally take the form of either tablets or crystalline powder. Recently an illegal, smokable form of methamphetamine known as *ice* has been appearing in certain areas of the United States, specifically Hawaii and the West Coast, where it seems to be gaining popularity as an alternative to crack cocaine.

Although it was synthesized in 1887, the first amphetamine—amphetamine sulfate—was not marketed in the United States until the early 1930s. It was sold in the form of an inhaler under the brand name of Benzedrine for use as a nasal decongestant and as a treatment for asthma. Later, when its powerful stimulant properties were discovered, amphetamine sulfate was sold in tablet form to treat depression, decrease fatigue, and curb the appetite. During World War II, amphetamines were distributed to British, Japanese, and German forces to increase their endurance and improve their fighting performance. During the Korean War, the United States began supplying its troops with amphetamines for the same purpose.

Sometimes prescribed in the treatment of narcolepsy, a sleep disorder, amphetamines are also the active ingredients of many preparations for promoting wakefulness and as aids for suppressing the appetite.

Amphetamines were widely prescribed during the 1950s and 1960s, and it was not until the 1960s that their abuse began to cause great concern. New federal regulations limiting the use of amphetamines were introduced in 1971, but because these drugs are fairly simple to make, illegal supplies remained available.

Unlike cocaine, a stimulant whose effects last for only 30 to 60 minutes, the effects of amphetamines may last from 4 to 12 hours, depending on the type and dosage of the drug. The potent, long-lasting stimulant properties of amphetamines have made them popular among college students who want to stay awake to prepare for examinations and workers who must endure lengthy shifts. Substance abusers often use amphetamines to counteract the effects of alcohol or other depressant drugs or to alleviate the *crash* or sharp decline in mood and energy that follows a cocaine or crack binge.

Because amphetamines and similar stimulants diminish appetite, heavy users of these drugs often suffer from vitamin deficiencies and other forms of malnutrition. These conditions can lead to more serious health problems. Amphetamines also increase blood pressure, which makes them particularly dangerous to persons with heart problems or blood pressure that is already high.

Amphetamines and other stimulants can cause sleeplessness, irritability, confusion, physical weakness, fatigue, anxiety, and severe—often suicidal—depression. The use of amphetamines for long periods or in high doses has in some cases caused symptoms of paranoid psychosis, including delirium, abnormal suspiciousness, and delusions of power, sometimes accompanied by hallucinations. These symptoms usually subside when use of the causative drug is discontinued.

The prolonged use of amphetamines can induce tolerance, leading long-term abusers to consume massive doses that would be fatal to a nonuser. The repeated use of amphetamines can also create a strong psychological dependence. Withdrawal from amphetamines generally entails physical and mental fatigue, sleepiness, and depression lasting two to three days. In extreme cases, treatment for amphetamine abuse may include detoxification in a hospital. The chronic depression that can affect recovering amphetamine abusers is often addressed through outpatient counseling or psychotherapy.

CHAPTER 4

MARIJUANA/PCP/ PSYCHEDELICS/ DESIGNER DRUGS

Covered with artistic designs, these squares of blotting paper have been impregnated with LSD. This is a common method of ingesting the substance.

The NIDA 1990 Household Survey found that marijuana was the third most widely used psychoactive drug in the United States, after alcohol and cigarettes (and discounting caffeinated beverages). One third of all Americans age 12 and older—an estimated 66 million persons—had used it at least once, and the survey found more than 10 million current users. Unlike alcohol and tobacco, however, marijuana use is illegal in the United States and many other parts of the world, except for licensed medical use. While statistics show that the use of marijuana has decreased substantially in the United States since the late 1970s, its continued popularity remains a source of controversy and concern.

Marijuana

Also known as pot, herb, *ganja*, and by various other names, marijuana is made from the flowering tops and leaves of *Cannabis sativa* (or Indian hemp), a weed that grows throughout many parts of the world, including North America. The *Cannabis* plant has been farmed for thousands of years for a variety of purposes, among them the manufacture of cloth, rope, and paper (from the plant's fibrous stalks); as a source of cereal, oil, and animal feed (from its seeds); and for the mood-altering properties of its leaves and flowers.

Of the many chemical compounds in marijuana, the one primarily responsible for marijuana's mood-altering effects is called delta-9 tetrahydrocannabinol, or THC. The potency of marijuana varies with

Hashish oil, a highly concentrated derivative of the Cannabis *plant. As much as 60% of the oil may consist of delta-9 tetrahydrocannabinol, or THC, the main ingredient in marijuana.*

the amount of THC it contains, which can range from 1% to 10% or more. Various factors will affect the THC content of marijuana, and many of those who grow the plant have developed techniques of cultivation designed to maximize the potency of the drug. The form of marijuana known as *sinsemilla* (meaning "without seeds"), for instance, generally consists of mature female flowers, which can have an extremely high THC content.

Hashish is a processed form of marijuana generally made by thrashing *Cannabis* plants over a screen and compacting the remaining resinous material into a puttylike mass. It is commonly found in India, the Middle East, and parts of northern Africa, from where it is often smuggled into Europe and the United States. The THC content of hashish may vary from 1% to over 12%. Less commonly encountered is hash oil, a highly concentrated extract made from *Cannabis* flowers, which can have from 1% to as much as 60% THC.

While marijuana is sometimes eaten in food (usually cookies or brownies) or made into a tea, it is most often consumed by smoking.

Marijuana cigarettes
are known as joints,
reefers, or spliffs.

49

Users will either roll dried marijuana shreds into a cigarette—referred to as a *joint*, *spliff*, or *reefer*—or smoke them in a conventional or water-cooled pipe. The smoke is generally inhaled deep into the lungs and held there for a few moments to maximize its effects. Hashish and hash oil are often mixed with tobacco or marijuana and smoked in a similar fashion.

Marijuana affects people in different ways, ranging from no influence on some first-time users to deep relaxation in others and feelings of agitation and alienation in still others. Its variable effects can be attributed to a number of factors, including the amount and the potency of the drug and the user's mood and expectations before using it.

Generally, marijuana that is smoked acts in two stages. The first usually begins within a few minutes and can last from 30 minutes to an hour or more. It is usually characterized by a jumbled rush of ideas and an intensified perception of sound, color, taste, scent, and touch. The second phase usually consists of relaxation or sleepiness and can last from two to three hours or more. Additionally, marijuana may increase the appetite and may produce a dryness of the mouth. The effects of eating marijuana are similar to those of smoking it, except that they begin more slowly and generally last longer.

History of Marijuana

Cannabis is one of the oldest agricultural crops known to humankind. Although its use as a food and fiber plant was established earlier, the mood-altering use of marijuana was first documented in China in the *Pe-ts'ao Ching*, the world's oldest pharmacopoeia, believed to have been written around 2800 B.C. Research also indicates that the Aryan culture of India used marijuana for relaxation and in religious rituals prior to 1000 B.C., and its use played a role in both Sufi and Tibetan religious traditions as well.

Hemp was an important fiber crop in the United States from the mid-1600s to the late 1800s, after which it was displaced by domestic cotton and imported fibers. The practice of smoking marijuana was first introduced by Mexican and Caribbean laborers in the southern states during the late 19th and early 20th century, where its use soon spread.

At the same time, hashish smoking had become popular in certain nothern cities, such as New York and Chicago, after Turkish merchants introduced the practice at international expositions. Furthermore, many physicians of the time used marijuana for treating headaches, insomnia, menstrual cramps, and other ailments, and it was available in a variety of forms in most drug stores.

Public concern over the use of marijuana developed largely as a result of sensationalized and often wildly exaggerated stories about the drug's dangers. Tales of brutal murders committed by persons under the influence of marijuana appeared in newspapers across the country. Most historians acknowledge that these stories grew out of racist sentiment toward the Mexican and Caribbean immigrants who commonly used the drug; passing laws to prohibit its use was a means of justifying the harassment of newcomers.

Between 1914 and 1931, 29 states passed laws that made marijuana use illegal. In 1937, despite objections by the American Medical Association and the pharmaceutical industry that marijuana was apparently both safe and medically useful, Congress passed the Marijuana Tax Act, largely as a result of pressure by some law-enforcement officials who wanted a federal marijuana law on the books. This effectively outlawed marijuana use in the United States.

In the mid-1960s, marijuana became connected with the so-called counterculture movement, and its use increased dramatically in the United States. During the late 1960s and 1970s, many groups, and even President Jimmy Carter, advocated eliminating criminal penalties for using the drug. As a result, many states amended their marijuana laws during the 1970s, reducing penalties for the use and possession of small amounts of marijuana to moderate fines (less than $200 in most cases) that were generally levied in the form of traffic tickets. In the 1980s, however, tolerance toward the use of marijuana waned as the nation reaffirmed its commitment to eradicating drug use of all kinds.

Marijuana and Health

The true health risks involved in using marijuana remain unclear. Many advocates claim that moderate use of marijuana is safe. In fact, after two years of court hearings intended to establish the value of marijuana as a medicinal drug, Francis Young, chief judge of the U.S. Drug Enforcement Administration, concluded in 1989 that marijuana was "one of the safest therapeutically active substances known to man." Yet a sizable amount of research indicates that the use of marijuana may be connected to a variety of medical problems.

For instance, marijuana is known to increase the heart rate, and its use can therefore increase stress on the cardiovascular system. Some research also indicates that its use may temporarily impair the body's immune system, weakening its defenses against virus-caused and other diseases. Marijuana has also been shown to affect the hormonal system and is believed to impair fertility in some people.

Beyond this, marijuana smoke, like tobacco smoke, contains a number of harmful compounds. Studies have shown that it contains from three to five times more of the toxic gas carbon monoxide than cigarette smoke, along with at least three times more tar. Frequent smoking of marijuana irritates various parts of the respiratory system, including the upper and lower airways, trachea, bronchi, larynx, and sinuses, and can result in a cough or sore throat. Heavy marijuana smoking has also been linked to the development of precancerous lesions in the lungs, although no definite connection has been established between lung cancer and marijuana smoking.

The psychological effects of marijuana have been another topic of considerable debate. The use of marijuana can impair coordination and concentration, thus increasing the risk involved in operating motor vehicles and other machinery. Marijuana smoking has also been shown to impair short-term memory, an effect that can apparently last for weeks after frequent users have stopped smoking. Another condition linked to chronic marijuana use is an amotivational syndrome characterized by apathy, lack of ambition, diminished physical activity, and certain forms of self-neglect. However, whether frequent marijuana use causes this syndrome or whether persons with such personality traits are simply more likely to become frequent marijuana users has not been conclusively established.

Psychological dependence on marijuana has been shown to occur among frequent marijuana users, and withdrawal symptoms, including irritability, loss of appetite, sleeplessness, and nausea, have been noted when persons who regularly smoke more than five marijuana cigarettes daily stop using the drug abruptly. Tolerance to marijuana can develop with its frequent use, although researchers disagree on how and to what extent this occurs. Habitual marijuana users seeking to quit may turn to self-help groups, such as Potsmokers Anonymous or Narcotics Anonymous, or to other forms of counseling and psychotherapy.

The evidence that marijuana has certain unique medicinal properties further clouds the issue of its use. It has proven effective for treating glaucoma, a progressive vision disorder, and for alleviating nausea associated with various forms of chemotherapy for cancer. Yet it remains an extremely difficult process to obtain legal marijuana in the United States for medical purposes. Such groups as the Alliance for Cannabis Therapeutics (ACT) and the National Organization for the Reform of Marijuana Laws (NORML) have lobbied extensively to allow disease sufferers easier access to the drug.

On the whole, there is little agreement on the topic of marijuana use and a marked shortage of reliable information. Addiction researcher Dr. Mark S. Gold asserts that most of the studies done on marijuana use over the past thirty years were done by researchers with somewhat biased notions of what they wanted to find, and the late substance abuse expert Dr. Sidney Cohen of the University of California at Los Angeles observed that it is possible to selectively cite research to back up any opinion about the drug, pro or con. More objective, long-term research is needed to establish the true health risks of marijuana use.

Hallucinogens

Drugs such as *lysergic acid diethylamide-25* (LSD), *peyote* (along with its derivative, mescaline), and *psilocybin* mushrooms are classified as *hallucinogens* or psychedelic agents. These are powerful psychoactive drugs without any recognized medical application, and under most circumstances their use remains illegal in the United States.

LSD, also known as acid, is an odorless, colorless liquid derived from ergot, a fungus that is found on rye and other grasses. It is most often taken orally and sold in the form of small squares of blotter paper (referred to simply as blotter) into which it has been absorbed, or in gelatin squares (known as window pane) onto which it has been applied; the former may be decorated with cartoon characters or some other identifying trademark. LSD is also applied to sugar cubes or sold in the form of tiny, saccharine-like tablets (often called microdots). An LSD experience, or trip, may last from 6 to 12 hours.

Peyote is the term generally used to describe the fleshy center, or button, of the peyote cactus, which grows in arid climates in Mexico

Various species of mushrooms of the genus Psilocybe. *Grown in the wild or cultivated, the mushrooms are eaten in fresh or dried form to obtain the hallucinogenic effects of the substance psilocybin, which they contain.*

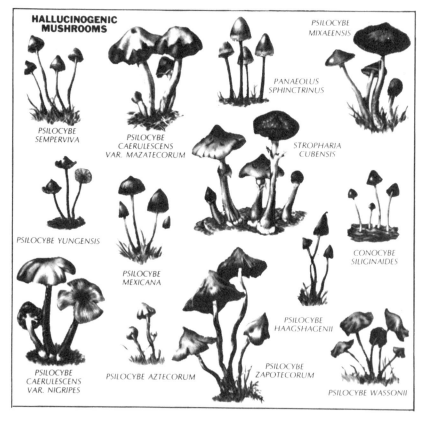

and other areas. It is usually eaten in fresh or dried form, often in combination with food or drink that can serve to mask its extremely bitter and unpleasant taste. Its effects may last from 5 to 12 hours.

Mescaline, the main psychoactive chemical in peyote, can be produced synthetically and is generally sold in the form of small pills or powder. The mushrooms that contain psilocybin (also known as *magic mushrooms*) grow wild throughout the United States and other parts of the world; they can also be cultivated indoors. Like peyote, they are eaten in fresh or dried form and have a vaguely unpleasant taste. The effects of psilocybin generally last from 3 to 6 hours, depending on the quantity eaten.

The specific ways in which psychedelic drugs act on the mind are unknown, and it is difficult to precisely describe their effects. Physically, hallucinogens generally increase the heart and respiratory rates and often cause nausea and muscle weakness. Psychologically, these drugs can produce visual distortions that may include an altered perception of color and light intensity, along with the sensation that static objects are moving.

Synesthesia, the sensation that one can "hear" colors or "see" music, has been reported by some users of hallucinogens, as have distorted perceptions of time and space. The emotional effects of psychedelic drugs can be extremely intense, ranging from profound joy through feelings of spiritual and intellectual illumination and euphoria to overwhelming panic and paranoia, often referred to as a bad trip.

The use of peyote, psilocybin mushrooms, and other hallucinogens goes back hundreds, if not thousands, of years. Hallucinogenic mushrooms are known to have played a central part in the culture of the Aztecs of Central America, and groups native to North America, such as the Navaho Indians and the Kiowa-Apache, still use peyote in certain religious ceremonies.

The use of LSD began much more recently. This drug was first synthesized by Albert Hoffman, a Swiss chemist, in 1938. He discovered its powerful psychoactive properties five years later, when he accidently ingested a small amount of the drug. LSD was first used in the United States during the 1950s by psychiatric researchers, who hoped that it would be beneficial for treating mental illness. During the same period, the U.S. Army and Central Intelligence Agency became interested in its potential use as an agent of chemical warfare or as truth serum. These agencies conducted secret experiments with LSD that often involved giving it to civilians and enlisted men without their knowledge, a practice that later prompted many lawsuits against these agencies by the persons involved.

It was during the mid-1960s that LSD and other psychedelic drugs became popular for their psychoactive properties. Advocates of LSD, such as Dr. Timothy Leary, a Harvard psychologist who had conducted numerous experiments with hallucinogens, promoted its quasi-religious use as a way of freeing the mind and reaching a higher level of consciousness. During this period, the use of LSD was associated with ongoing protests against the war in Vietnam and with various counterculture movements, and it influenced much of the popular art and music of the period, which is still referred to as the psychedelic era.

Although the use of hallucinogens declined from the late 1970s to the mid-1980s, their popularity has recently shown a slight resurgence among persons under the age of 26, according to NIDA statistics. Overall, an estimated 15.3 million Americans have used some form of hallucinogen at least once; among persons aged 12 to 25, NIDA estimates that more than 400,000 are current users.

As previously mentioned, the major danger in the use of a hallucinogen is a panic reaction or bad trip. Studies have shown that the setting in which the drug is used, the user's expectations of its effects, and the user's mood before taking the drug all play a large part in determining the quality of the experience. A person in a positive state of mind and familiar, nonthreatening environment is less likely to have a panic reaction than someone who takes a hallucinogen under adverse circumstances.

The treatment for a negative experience with a hallucinogenic drug includes a quiet, dimly lit environment with a therapist whom the patient can trust and who can provide reassurance until the effects of the drug wear off. In extreme cases, mild tranquilizers such as diazepam (Valium) may be used to help calm the patient down.

Hallucinogens can produce a moderate psychological dependence in some users but do not appear to induce physical dependence or withdrawal. With frequent use, tolerance to their effects develops rapidly, but also subsides rapidly.

Because such hallucinogens as LSD and mescaline are produced illegally, neither their purity nor their potency can be readily determined. Some samples of LSD and mescaline have included varying amounts of amphetamines as well as PCP (see below), both of which may have adverse effects of their own.

Phencyclidine (PCP)

PCP is an unusual and potentially dangerous drug that can have the characteristics of a hallucinogen, sedative, or stimulant. Originally tested on humans for its anesthetic properties in the 1950s, its unpredictable aftereffects ended its medical use in the early 1960s, and it later became available from street dealers. PCP is sold in the form of pills (often marketed as THC, LSD, mescaline, or other substances), mixed with treated marijuana, tobacco, parsley, or mint leaves (known as angel dust) for smoking, snorting, or even injecting.

PCP can cause an alcohol-like intoxication characterized by loss of coordination and numbness; it may also cause fits of anxiety, agitation, confusion, distorted visual and auditory sensation, and in some cases violent psychotic reactions. PCP-induced psychosis has been known to last for days or even weeks following use of the drug. Although PCP is not physically addictive, it can be used chronically, and high doses have caused convulsions, coma, and death.

Ecstasy/Designer Drugs

Certain designer drugs, also known as analogs because they are derived from or modeled after legitimate prescription and other drugs, have somewhat different effects from those of their prototypes and are marketed illegally. *Methylenedioxymethamphetamine* (also known as *MDMA, ecstasy,* and *X*) achieved publicity during the early 1980s, when its use in legitimate psychotherapy was reputed to produce remarkable breakthroughs in communication and understanding between patients and their therapists, spouses, and families. Outlawed in 1985 because it was already being abused, it soon became a popular drug among college students and young adults in both the United States and abroad.

Chemically, MDMA is related to the amphetamines. Its effects are reported to include an increased heart rate, muscle tightness, mild visual hallucinations, and numbness in certain parts of the body. It has been reported to produce feelings of euphoria, along with a sense of empathy and connectedness with others (the latter an effect that has earned it the nickname of "the love drug"). It is also reputed to cause anxiety and confusion in some persons.

Preliminary animal research on MDMA indicates that it may damage certain brain cells and in large doses may be toxic in other ways. However, little is known about its potential dangers and long-term effects.

Enterprising chemists, often working clandestinely, seem to continually produce new forms of mood-altering drugs. Ultimately, it is the consumer of these drugs who becomes the guinea pig in ill-controlled experiments on their effects. The illegal drug market knows no such thing as quality control, and the effects of drugs—often unpredictable to begin with—become even harder to estimate in the presence of adulterants or false labeling. Illicit drug use always carries a risk.

CHAPTER 5

COCAINE/CRACK

A typical cocaine-growing area in a mountainous region of Bolivia.

The explosive growth of cocaine use during the 1970s, followed by the popularization of crack cocaine in the 1980s, put the spotlight on cocaine as perhaps the most threatening of abused substances. While it is not physically addictive in the same way as opiates, alcohol, or barbiturates, cocaine can induce a psychological dependence of such intensity that its acquisition and use become the most important things in the user's life. Although NIDA reports noted a sharp decrease in overall cocaine use in the United States between

1985 and 1990, crack and cocaine abuse still constitute a major part of the nation's drug problem.

Properties of Cocaine

The coca plant (*Erythroxylon coca*), from which cocaine is derived, is a shrub that grows predominantly in mountainous regions of South and Central America. Indian groups in Peru and Bolivia commonly chew the leaves of the plant, which contain approximately 1% cocaine, for their stimulant effect, much as Americans drink coffee or tea.

From 250 to 500 kilograms of coca leaves are needed to produce a single kilogram of pure cocaine. The conversion process involves treating the leaves with a variety of chemicals, which may include kerosene, sulfuric acid, hydrochloric acid, ether, acetone, and ammonia. The procedure is fairly complex and is usually performed in hidden, makeshift laboratories located near where the coca plant is grown.

In its pure form, cocaine hydrochloride, the product of the conversion process, is a white, odorless, crystalline powder that has two main pharmacological characteristics. The first is an anesthetic property that numbs or "freezes" body tissue that comes into contact with the drug. In this function, cocaine is similar to novocaine or xylocaine, two

Coca leaves ready for processing into cocaine. From 250 to 500 kilograms of these leaves are needed to produce a kilogram of pure cocaine.

related drugs often used to provide anesthesia for dental procedures. Cocaine itself is occasionally still used as an anesthetic in certain types of nose and eye surgery.

Cocaine's other characteristic property—and the one for which it is generally abused—is its stimulation of the central nervous system, which creates a feeling of euphoria and heightened energy. While its exact mechanism is unknown, scientists believe that cocaine stimulates the production of certain neurotransmitters, or chemical messengers, in the brain and prolongs their actions. Norepinephrine and dopamine are two neurotransmitters affected by cocaine.

Cocaine's stimulant properties affect other parts of the body besides the brain. The drug increases heart and respiration (breathing) rates, blood pressure, and body temperature. It also causes the tightening or narrowing of blood vessels in the body, an action known as vasoconstriction.

Like all drugs sold illicitly, street cocaine is very often diluted, or *cut*, with less expensive substances to increase its bulk and thus its value (cocaine is most often sold by weight). Stimulants such as amphetamines and caffeine, along with lidocaine or other anesthetics, are commonly used for this purpose because they mimic the effects of cocaine. Inert ingredients such as cornstarch, dextrose, talcum powder, and other materials are added to increase the weight and volume of the cocaine. In general, what is sold on the street as cocaine ranges from 50% to less than 20% cocaine hydrochloride. Cocaine users can therefore never be sure of exactly what they are putting into their bodies.

History

Archaeologists have found coca leaves among the artifacts in Peruvian gravesites dating back to about A.D. 500, implying that the use of coca leaves for their mood-altering effects is at least 1,500 years old. Records of the Inca civilization, discovered in the area of what is now Bolivia and Peru, suggest the practice may be twice as old as that.

The modern Peruvian and Bolivian Indians' custom of chewing coca leaves is the continuation of an ancient tradition (according to one source, 9 million kilograms of coca leaves are consumed yearly in Peru alone). It serves to energize workers who labor in the high altitudes of the Andes Mountains, where oxygen is scarce and exhaustion is rapid. It also acts to suppress appetite, an important function among impoverished tribes where food is often scarce.

Cocaine hydrochloride was first isolated from the coca plant by Friedrich Gaedecke, a German chemist, in 1855. Scientists and others soon became intensely interested in the drug, prompting research into its effects and a great deal of experimentation with the drug. Among the first and most famous investigators of the effects of cocaine was Sigmund Freud, the founder of psychoanalysis. Freud did this both by observation of others and by taking the drug himself. In 1884 he published "On Cocaine", a landmark paper that praised the drug at length for its pharmaceutical properties. Freud claimed that cocaine could be used as an effective treatment for depression and other types of mental illness and that it could release alcoholics and morphine addicts from their addictions.

Unfortunately, Freud's enthusiasm for cocaine was based more on personal prejudice than on scientific research, and many members of the scientific community accused him of irresponsibility in his unqualified promotion of the drug. He later modified his views on the drug as more information about it became available.

Meanwhile, cocaine became a popular ingredient in various patent medicines and kept this role into the early 1900s. In 1863, an Italian chemist named Anghelo Mariani created a concoction known as Vin Mariani, prepared from a mixture of wine and coca leaves. The product was greeted enthusiastically, with its users including American scientist Thomas Edison and French writer Jules Verne. Cocaine was also added to other products, including cigarettes and soft drinks. In 1886, an American chemist named John Styth Pemberton developed a patent medicine that contained cocaine. It would later be marketed as a soft drink under the brand name Coca-Cola. After the beverage had been on the market for some years, caffeine replaced cocaine as its active ingredient, but coca leaves (with the cocaine removed) are still used today in flavoring Coca-Cola.

Eventually, the tide of public opinion turned against cocaine. During the early 1900s, the press began to link its use to criminal

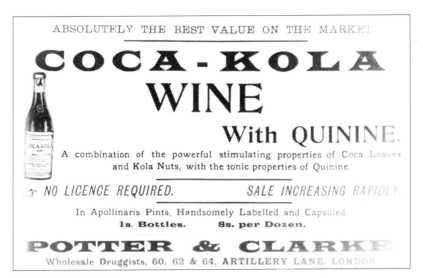

During the late 19th and early 20th centuries, cocaine became a popular ingredient in many patent medicines in the United States and Europe. One of them was the combination of coca leaves, kola nuts, quinine, and wine shown here and marketed under the name Coca-Kola.

behavior in varied and often sensational reports. The press also began a campaign that challenged the usefulness of patent medicines generally, many of which were sold under grossly exaggerated claims of effectiveness. As this happened, further evidence was accumulating of cocaine's highly addictive nature. All of these factors finally led Congress to pass the Harrison Act in 1914, which outlawed the use of cocaine without a prescription.

After the Harrison Act, the use of cocaine in the United States subsided and did not revive until the late 1960s, when many psychoactive drugs were becoming more popular. The so-called cocaine epidemic of the 1970s is usually attributed to a number of causes, including the greater willingness of people to experiment with various mood-altering drugs during that era and the increased production and importation of cocaine into the United States. A third factor in the growth of cocaine abuse was the mystique surrounding the drug, fueled by reports of celebrity cocaine parties and the $75- to $100-per-gram price of the drug, which made it a status symbol.

But perhaps the main reason so many people were willing to try cocaine was the widespread belief that it was safe and nonaddictive. Both views have since proven incorrect, with often tragic consequences.

Methods of Use

Inhaling cocaine powder into the nostrils—a practice known as snorting, is perhaps the most common method of using cocaine. To prepare the drug for snorting, the user generally places it on a flat, smooth, nonporous surface, such as a small mirror or glass tabletop. Because cocaine is a crystalline substance, a razor blade is often used to chop it into a fine powder and divide it into portions, or lines. The drug is then inhaled through a straw or rolled-up dollar bill or scooped into tiny spoons and sniffed into the nostrils.

When cocaine comes into contact with the lining of the nose, it is quickly absorbed through tiny blood vessels into the blood stream. It then travels through the circulatory system to the heart and ultimately to the brain. The cocaine high, or sense of elation, is usually felt from 3 to 5 minutes after snorting the drug, reaches a peak after 15 to 20 minutes, and subsides after 30 to 60 minutes. Many users experience a period of irritability, anxiety, or depression after taking cocaine—a syndrome known as *crashing*.

In addition to being inhaled, cocaine can also be taken intravenously. In this case, cocaine powder is mixed with a small amount of water, strained, drawn into a hypodermic needle, and injected directly into the user's vein. When it is injected, the effects of the drug are felt almost instantly, and the high is of greater intensity than when it is snorted. However, the high usually lasts only 5 minutes and subsides after 15 to 20 minutes.

Cocaine that has been converted into its *free base* or *crack* form by removing the hydrochloride from the drug can be smoked. Without this conversion the heat of a flame would destroy cocaine hydrochloride without producing any euphoric effects in the user. Crack smokers usually use a small, hand-held glass pipe. They may also mix crack with tobacco or marijuana and smoke it in cigarette form. Cocaine that

The name crack *refers to cocaine that has been converted to its free-base form by means of baking soda (left), ammonia (right), or other nonflammable substances. Taking the form of waxlike chips or pebbles for smoking, crack is highly addictive but has only short-lived effects.*

is smoked is rapidly absorbed into the bloodstream, traveling to the brain faster and in a greater concentration than when it is snorted or injected and generally producing an effect within 10 seconds. As with injecting cocaine, however, the high from smoking cocaine, although more intense, is also shorter-lived than that from snorting the drug; it peaks within two to five minutes and is generally over within twenty minutes, with an ensuing crash that is likewise of greater intensity.

When the practice of smoking cocaine was first introduced to users in the United States during the mid-1970s, users generally had to convert their own cocaine to the freebase form. This was a complicated and often dangerous endeavor that involved the use of ether, a highly combustible fluid. Many persons, including a few well-known ones, were injured, sometimes seriously. The name *crack* was born in the early 1980s when a simplified method of freebasing cocaine, using baking soda rather than ether, was developed. Unlike conventional cocaine or freebase, crack takes the form of small, waxlike beige chips or pebbles rather than a white powder or crystals. Although one or two small pieces, enough for a single high, may cost as little as $5, an addiction to crack can cost hundreds of dollars a day.

The freebasing of cocaine—in which it is converted into a form that can be smoked—was originally a highly dangerous process requiring the use of ether and other combustible fluids. Among the many persons injured during freebasing was comedian Richard Pryor, who has since regained his health.

Spacebasing, Speedballing, and Basuco

As noted earlier, cocaine is sometimes mixed with other drugs in order to increase or modify its effects. Thus, crack that has been treated with phencyclidine (PCP or angel dust, as described in chapter 3), is said to have been spacebased, while the injection of cocaine mixed with heroin—done to counteract the powerful stimulant effect of cocaine alone—is known as *speedballing*. Because of the uncertain interactions of these two substances, this is a particularly dangerous practice.

By the same token, smoking *basuco*—a paste consisting of ground coca leaves along with some of the compounds used to extract cocaine from the leaves—can cause severe lung damage as well as the problems usually associated with cocaine use, since substances such as kerosene, gasoline, and sulphuric acid often remain in the paste.

Why Is Cocaine So Addictive?

As with most substances of abuse, cocaine is capable of producing a number of pleasant, mood-altering effects. It can increase a person's energy, self-confidence, alertness, and rate of mental activity. The cocaine user typically feels more powerful, talkative, and social than without the drug and may also experience increased sexual arousal. The desire for these effects is a strong element in cocaine abuse.

Another factor in the compulsive use of cocaine is the desire to alleviate the rebound or crash period that often follows a dose of the drug. In fact, many users will continue taking the drug relentlessly in a futile effort to avoid its negative aftereffects and maintain a high. When the supply of cocaine runs out, they often turn to other stimulants or alcohol to ease the inevitable crash.

Furthermore, tolerance to cocaine develops rapidly, and frequent users find that they must take larger and larger doses of the drug to acheive the same effect produced by their first, smaller doses. Chronic users may reach a point at which massive doses of cocaine fail to produce any pleasurable effects at all.

Because cessation of its use does not cause the pronounced symptoms characteristic of opiate or alcohol withdrawal, cocaine is not generally considered physically addictive. But some research suggests that its continued use may alter the brain in such a way as to contribute to its obsessive use. Dependence on cocaine, whether physical or mental, can occur much more rapidly than addiction to alcohol; for example, some crack users claim to have become addicted after only a single experience with the drug.

Addiction to cocaine can be devastating—tens of thousands of previously responsible persons have lost their jobs, relationships, and belongings in the process of feeding this costly and dangerous habit.

Treatment for cocaine addiction generally occurs in a substance-abuse rehabilitation program and involves detoxification, complete abstinence from other illegal drugs and alcohol, and changes in lifestyle (see chapter 7).

Medical Risks

The use of cocaine carries many health risks. Perhaps foremost is the danger of overdose, which can produce a variety of medical complications, some of them fatal. Because cocaine makes the heart beat faster, it may disturb the rhythm of the heart. Ventricular tachycardia (an extremely rapid heartbeat) or ventricular fibrillation (an extremely weak and irregular heartbeat) are two dangerous syndromes that may result from an overdose of cocaine. Because cocaine increases a person's blood pressure, an overdose may also cause a cerebral hemorrhage—the bursting of a blood vessel with the escape of blood into the brain, which can precipitate a stroke—or a heart attack, as in the case of 21-year-old University of Maryland basketball star Len Bias, who died from a cocaine-induced heart attack in 1986. Cocaine use can also cause respiratory failure, hyperpyrexia (increased body temperature), and epileptic seizures in some individuals.

One factor that contributes to the likelihood of overdose is the uncertain potency of street cocaine; it is difficult to know just how

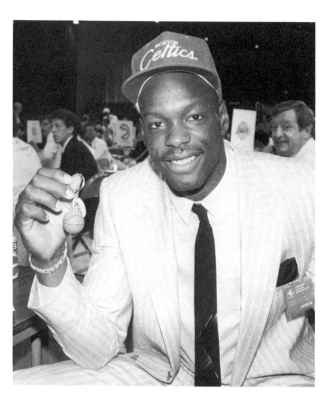

Former University of Maryland basketball player Len Bias. A talented athlete heading toward a career in professional basketball, Bias died of a cocaine-induced heart attack in 1986.

much pure cocaine a street consumer is putting into his or her body at any one time. Another factor is that tolerance to cocaine's effects leads users to take larger and larger amounts of the drug to achieve the desired high. How much cocaine is too much? It is difficult to say. The increased sensitivity of many chronic users to some of cocaine's effects (known as the kindling phenomenon) makes the risk of overdose even greater.

Finally, some persons are simply more susceptible than others to medical problems caused by cocaine. The usual dose for one person may prove lethal to another. It is therefore difficult to know exactly how anyone will react to even a small amount of the drug. Besides its effect on the heart, cocaine can create a host of health problems. Snorting it can seriously damage the mucous membrane lining the nose, causing nosebleeds and nasal ulcers. In severe cases, a break or perforation in the nasal septum—the portion of the nose that separates the two nostrils—can occur. Smoking cocaine has been shown to cause various types of lung damage, both from the cocaine itself and from the various adulterants that it may contain. Both snorting and smoking cocaine suppress the appetite, and heavy users often suffer from malnutrition.

The user who injects cocaine faces a further set of risks. The sharing of unsterile hypodermic needles by intravenous drug users is among the foremost ways in which AIDS is transmitted. Other infections that can stem from injecting cocaine are hepatitis (an inflammation of the liver), endocarditis (an infection of the heart valve), and various skin infections (diseases directly related to intravenous drug use are discussed at greater length in chapter 6).

The effects of cocaine and crack on the unborn children of pregnant mothers have recently been documented. They can include premature birth, a low birth weight, and various birth defects. Moreover, learning disabilities and behavioral disorders have been observed among children exposed to cocaine before birth. According to a 1989 White House report, approximately 100,000 *cocaine babies* are born each year to mothers who use the drug during pregnancy.

The Societal Costs of Cocaine Use

Because cocaine is both expensive (heavy users may spend hundreds of dollars a day on the drug) and illegal, a huge criminal network has grown up around its manufacture and sale. The coca plant can grow only in certain climates, such as those found in Colombia, Peru, and Bolivia. As a result, the groups that control the production of cocaine in these countries—often known as cartels—have vast wealth and power, which they often use to terrorize the local populace and even the government.

During the 1970s, cocaine use in the United States was primarily an upper-class phenomenon because of the high cost of the drug. With the introduction of crack cocaine—which is generally sold in smaller, less expensive quantities—to the inner city in the early 1980s, the market for the drug grew enormously. With that growth came a new breed of illegal drug merchants: rival "businessmen" and young gangs involved in selling the drug. Because the stakes are high, these distributors defend their sales territories fiercely. Shootouts, often harming innocent bystanders, are not uncommon in some areas. An increase in various forms of theft also seems to accompany the rise of crack use in a neighborhood, as addicts seek to finance insatiable drug habits. The advent of crack houses—urban buildings that are taken over by drug dealers so that they can provide customers with drugs, drug paraphernalia, and a place where the users can smoke crack undetected, is another trend connected with cocaine.

To many, the rise in popularity of cocaine and crack epitomizes the drug problem in the United States. While NIDA figures show fewer Americans using cocaine, those who are using it are doing so with great frequency; in 1990, an estimated 662,000 persons were using cocaine one or more times a week. Furthermore, NIDA research also shows a doubling in the reported number of deaths from cocaine between the end of 1986 and the beginning of 1989. Clearly, the nation's cocaine problem is far from solved.

CHAPTER 6

HEROIN/OPIATES

The opium poppy, Papaver somniferum. *As the source of opium, it is also the origin of heroin and all other natural opiates.*

The term *opiate* refers to any drug derived from opium, the dried juice of the opium poppy plant, *Papaver somniferum.* The term is also used to describe certain synthetic drugs that are chemically similar to the true opiates. The term *narcotic*, often used incorrectly as a blanket description for a wide variety of illicit drugs, is synonomous with the term opiate.

Opium is one of the oldest drugs known to man, and the medical profession still uses opium-based preparations on a large scale for treating severe cases of pain, diarrhea, and coughing. Yet the powerful euphoric effects of opiate drugs have always given them a high potential for abuse, and their abuse inevitably carries the risk of physical addiction.

What Opium Is and What It Does

In its crude form, opium is a brownish black, gummy substance obtained from the ripened pods of the opium poppy. Like the coca plant, the opium poppy thrives only in specific climates. The so-called Golden Crescent region of the Middle East (which includes parts of Afghanistan, Iran, and Pakistan) and the Golden Triangle of Indonesia and parts of Laos, Myanmar, and Thailand produce a large share of the world's opium supply.

Although in the past opium was used mainly in its crude form, it is now more commonly taken in the form of refined opiate drugs such as *morphine*, *heroin*, and *codeine*. Crude or refined, all opiates share certain basic characteristics.

First, opiates depress the central nervous system. They also alter the way an individual perceives pain; in this capacity, they have been

A field of opium poppies growing in northern Mexico. Most of the world's opium comes from the Golden Crescent area of the Middle East, which includes parts of Afghanistan, Iran, and Pakistan, and the Golden Triangle of Indonesia and parts of Laos, Myanmar, and Thailand.

found to resemble closely the body's natural painkillers, the group of neurotransmitter chemicals known as endorphins, which act in the brain.

Endorphins are believed to control pain partly by moderating the emotions that accompany pain. Opiate drugs work in a similar way: they reduce anxiety and stress and produce drowsiness. Doctors have found that these drugs can temporarily reduce or eliminate pain in many patients.

Another effect of opiate drugs is to impede some kinds of muscle contractions. This makes morphine useful in treating severe diarrhea, since it restricts the muscular contractions known as peristalsis that move food through the digestive system. Similarly, the opiate known as codeine is often used in cough syrups because it suppresses the muscular contractions of the cough reflex. Opiate drugs can also cause nausea and constipation.

History

According to archaeological records, the use of opium may have been known to the Sumerians, in what is now Iraq, as long ago as 4000 B.C.

Opium and its effects have been known to humankind for thousands of years. In the 4th century B.C., *the Greek physician Hippocrates recommended using it to treat a variety of ailments.*

After a period of dormancy in Europe and the West, the use of opium was revived by the Swiss scientist Paracelsus, who promoted it—under the name laudanum—as a cure-all. By the late 1600s, opium had been adopted throughout Europe as a home remedy.

It was also known to the Assyrians, the Babylonians, and the ancient Egyptians; in fact, trade in opium is known to have been a substantial business during the height of early Egyptian culture in the 13th century B.C. Centuries later, in ancient Greece, Hippocrates (460–377 B.C.), called the father of modern medicine, advocated the use of opium for a variety of maladies.

Later, opium made its way into the Far East and Europe, through trade with the Arab world. In the West, its use was limited until the renowned Swiss scientist Paracelsus (1493–1541) promoted it—in the form of small black pills that he called laudanum—as a general cure-all, a kind of "wonder drug." After his death, followers of Paracelsus continued to praise the drug's qualities, and while its acceptance by the medical profession was still limited, its usefulness as a home remedy had become recognized throughout Europe by the late 17th century.

In China, the practice of smoking opium for its intoxicant effects became popular during the 17th and 18th centuries. This led to numerous unsuccessful attempts by the Chinese government to outlaw its use. Because the British, who were then the world's main opium merchants, depended heavily on revenue from opium sales in China (where they were selling more than 2 million pounds sterling worth a year by 1830), they were unwilling to comply with the Chinese government's requests to stop importing the drug. This conflict of interests led to the so-called Opium Wars between China and Great Britain, which occurred between 1839 and 1860. Although some historians claim the Opium Wars were less about opium than about the complexities of international trade agreements, they underscore the difficulty of prohibiting a drug trade that brings a large profit.

Although opium was long used in various preparations and elixirs, the first true opiate derivative was not discovered until 1803, when a 20-year-old German pharmacy student named Friedrich Sertuerner isolated what is now known as morphine from crude opium. Doctors were immediately enthusiastic about the drug, and their enthusiasm grew after the invention of the hypodermic syringe by Dr. Alexander Wood of Edinburgh in 1843. Injectable morphine was far more predictable in its effects than any previous opium preparation, and it began to be used widely for both pain relief and for treating insanity. Heroin, an even more potent opiate than morphine, was developed in England in 1874.

At first, the West paid little attention to the problem of opium addiction, mainly because the benefits of opium and morphine—medical and otherwise—were so impressive and because the two drugs were cheap and widely available. Opium addiction was first recognized as a problem in England during the early 1800s with its extensive non-medical use by the Fens, the natives of the northern region of England. Later, its use by various writers, notably Samuel Taylor Coleridge (a notorious opium addict who claimed to have composed his famous poem "Kubla Khan" while under the effects of the drug) and Thomas De Quincey (who published *Confessions of an English Opium Eater* in 1822) drew more attention to the issue.

In the United States, morphine was used extensively in battlefield hospitals during the Civil War. During this period, opium-based patent medicines also became widely available, and by the late 19th Century,

Chinese immigrants who came to the United States to work on the railroads had introduced the practice of smoking opium. It has been estimated that by 1900 as much as 1% of the nation was addicted to some form of narcotic.

In 1914, the Harrison Act outlawed the use of opium and all opiate preparations without a prescription. Nevertheless, the illicit use of narcotics has continued in fits and starts right up to the present. According to NIDA's 1990 Household Survey, more than 1.6 million Americans have tried heroin at least once in their lives, and the number of Americans addicted to the drug is generally estimated to be about 500,000. However, some health-care professionals believe that this number greatly underestimates the scope of heroin abuse, because the social stigma that it carries makes accurate data difficult to obtain.

Methods of Use

Opiate use varies with the form of the drug. Crude opium is generally smoked or eaten, but this form is rarely available in the United States. Pharmaceutical tablets containing morphine, codeine, or other opiates may be taken orally or ground into a powder that can be either inhaled into the nostrils or mixed with water and injected. Cough syrups containing codeine are also imbibed for their opiate effects.

Heroin remains the opiate of choice among most narcotics users because of its more potent euphoric effects. Although pure heroin takes the form of a white powder, heroin purchased on the street may range from white to pink, gray, or brown and may vary in consistency from a fine powder to a granular form resembling cat litter.

Although heroin can be smoked—a practice known among users as *chasing the dragon*—or snorted into the nostrils, as is cocaine, most users take it intravenously in order to achieve the greatest level of euphoria. The drug is dissolved in water in a spoon or other small container, and the mixture is heated over a small flame. The solution is then drawn into a hypodermic needle and injected directly into a vein. Following the injection, or hit, the user experiences a rush of pleasurable feelings, followed by a period of drowsy euphoria (often referred to as nodding) that can last several hours.

Regardless of how they take opiates, first-time users of these drugs will often experience severe nausea. This symptom generally disappears with continued use, but the latter can produce tolerance as well as both psychological and physical dependence on opiates, all of which are components of addiction.

Opiate Addiction

Generally speaking, no one who begins using a drug plans on becoming addicted. Although some persons may experiment with opiate drugs without developing a physical dependence on them, it is estimated that at least half of all opiate users will ultimately become addicted.

Physical dependence on an opiate occurs when, after prolonged and repeated use, the body becomes accustomed to its effects and requires a constant amount of the drug in order to maintain ordinary, normal sensations. Without it, the addict will experience painful withdrawal symptoms that may include nausea, abdominal cramps, sweating, trembling, aching muscles, weakness, irritability, loss of appetite, and an inability to sleep. This may occur after less than two weeks of frequent opiate use, regardless of whether the drug is eaten, smoked, or injected. Tolerance will also develop, with increasing doses of opiate needed to produce a "high." Most long-term addicts reach a point at which the opiates they take no longer make them high at all but function solely to prevent the discomfort of withdrawal.

The exact mechanism by which opiate addiction occurs is unknown. However, because opiates appear to mimic the effects of endorphins, some researchers believe that the continued use of opiates reduces the body's production of these "natural painkillers," requiring the addict to continue to use opiates merely to maintain a normal level of painkilling substances within the body. In fact, it has been suggested that persons whose bodies lack normal quantities of endorphin (perhaps because of a natural deficit of these substances) may be especially susceptible to opiate addiction as a substitute for the body's own missing endorphins.

Symptoms of withdrawal usually begin between 8 and 12 hours after the last use of an opiate drug and vary in intensity according to the amount of the drug the addict is accustomed to and the frequency with which the drug is taken. Thus, someone who uses heroin daily over a two-year period will generally experience more severe withdrawal symptoms than an addict who has been taking the drug three or four times a week over a six-month period. The withdrawal period may last several days, generally reaching its peak after 36 to 72 hours. Although unpleasant, opiate withdrawal is generally not fatal.

Medical Risks

In addition to producing nausea and constipation, the use of opiates can lead to more severe health problems. Because opiate abuse often causes a loss of appetite, frequent users often suffer from malnutrition. The prolonged use of opiates has also been shown to weaken the body's immune system, making it less able to defend itself against diseases.

Furthermore, the opiate addiction of a pregnant woman is transferred to her child. Sudden withdrawal from opiates by a pregnant woman can result in premature birth—opiates should therefore not be given up during pregnancy without the advice of a doctor.

The most severe threat presented by the use of opiates is that of overdose. As with cocaine and other drugs bought illicitly, the opiate user can never be sure of the purity or strength of the drug that he or she is taking, so that an overdose is a constant danger. A packet of heroin, for example, is likely to include any number of other materials, ranging from lactose or mannitol (two types of sugar), which do not generally present significant health risks, to flour or talc, which can lodge in the veins and create serious problems when injected. Quinine and other drugs (including some synthetic opiates that are many times stronger than heroin) are also used as cutting agents and have been blamed for many deaths among intravenous opiate abusers.

Because opiates decrease the rate of breathing, most deaths from overdose are attributed to *respiratory arrest* (cessation of breathing).

Although treatments have been developed for opiate overdose (including the use of naloxone, a drug that temporarily halts the effects of opiates on the body), it is still often fatal.

Unsanitary and improper injection of opiates can also lead to a wide variety of ailments. Among them are various skin problems, including abscesses or deep sores in the skin that develop at the body sites used for drug injection. Scarring may also result from frequent injections.

Addicts often use unsterile hypodermic needles to inject opiates, and they can get infectious diseases from bacteria and viruses present in these needles, especially those that have been used by others. Among the diseases commonly spread in this way are septicemia (blood poisoning), hepatitis B (an inflammation of the liver), endocarditis (an infection of the heart valve), and AIDS.

The risk of getting AIDS is a major danger of intravenous drug use. Other diseases spread by intravenous drug use include blood poisoning, hepatitis B, and endocarditis.

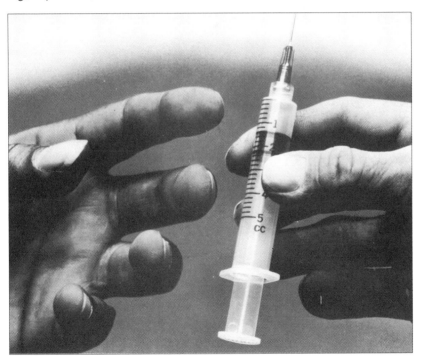

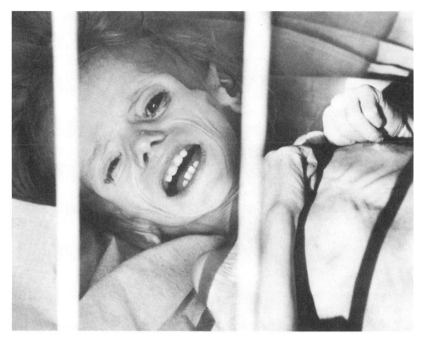

A nine-month-old infant dying of AIDS acquired from its mother before birth. Many infants afflicted with AIDS get the disease from a mother who has become infected through intravenous drug abuse before or during pregnancy.

AIDS and Intravenous Drug Use

AIDS is a disease characterized by a severe suppression of the body's immune system, such that even minor diseases and infections become lethal. Thus, AIDS-related deaths do not stem from AIDS itself but from diseases that attack the body after its immune system has been damaged. There is no known cure for AIDS, and it is invariably fatal.

The cause of AIDS is a virus known as the human immunodeficiency virus (HIV). This virus can only be spread through contact with bodily fluids of an infected person, which can happen during unprotected sexual activity (sex without a condom) and when an intravenous drug user injects himself or herself with a needle previously used by someone infected with the virus. Also, women infected with

HIV pass the virus on to their unborn children. As of January 1990, at least 28% of all known AIDS cases were among intravenous drug users.

Intravenous drug users who become infected with HIV can spread the disease to others by sharing needles, through sexual contact, and during pregnancy, as noted above. Among the many strategies now being employed to stop the spread of AIDS among intravenous drug users are an effort to help addicts give up drugs and enter treatment; programs to educate drug users about how AIDS is spread, emphasizing condom use and proper needle hygiene; and, in some communities, the distribution of sterile hypodermic needles to those who continue to use drugs intravenously.

Treating Opiate Addiction

The rise of AIDS among intravenous opiate (as well as other drug) abusers has strengthened the need for effective treatment for drug abuse. However, the nature of opiate addiction presents unique problems for rehabilitation.

The initial challenge for the opiate addict is to rid his or her system of the drug, a process known as *detoxification*. Because opiates produce physical dependence, the detoxification process is usually accompanied by symptoms of withdrawal. When detoxification takes place in a controlled environment, such as a hospital or treatment center, symptoms of opiate withdrawal can sometimes be reduced or controlled by the use of other drugs. One such drug is methadone, a synthetic opiate.

Developed in Germany during World War II as a substitute for morphine, which had become unavailable in that country, methadone does not produce the euphoria characteristic of heroin and other opiates. Instead, it blocks the euphoric effects of other opiates, thus discouraging their use by addicts. It can also, however, block withdrawal symptoms as it satisfies the addict's physical need for opiates. During detoxification, methadone is generally given in decreasing doses over a period of days, permitting the addict's body to adjust gradually to the absence of narcotics.

After the addict has successfully gone through the detoxification process, he or she faces the challenge of staying away from opiates for good. Many recovering addicts are unable to meet this challenge; despite the problems caused by their addiction, their desire to use opiates remains too strong to resist. Some research suggests that as many as 90% of opiate addicts who have stopped the habit return to narcotics use again after six months.

Some health-care professionals who believe that opiate addicts have either a natural deficiency of endorphins or a chemical imbalance brought on by their opiate abuse assert that supplying them with opiate drugs may be a reasonable method for treating them. In the late 1960s, the English government instituted a system in which addicts were registered with the government health system and supplied with heroin at a minimal cost. This presented some problems—including the transfer of heroin from registered addicts to others—and was largely phased out. Some addicts in England, the United States, and elsewhere can legally obtain regular doses of methadone to alleviate the effects of opiate withdrawal.

Some professionals feel that methadone can be used indefinitely to remedy endorphin imbalances in opiate addicts. Others, however, feel that it simply replaces one addiction with another (like all opiates, methadone is addictive), and it remains a controversial method of treatment (see chapter 7).

Although no one system of treating substance abuse is 100% effective, conquering an opiate addiction is not impossible. With the right support services, many people can and do succeed in overcoming their chemical dependence on these drugs.

CHAPTER 7

REHABILITATION/ TREATMENT

A law-enforcement officer destroying kegs of illegal liquor during the American era of Prohibition, from 1920 to 1933.

Substance abuse in a host of forms has challenged humankind for centuries. In 16th-century Britain, it took the shape of gin abuse. Among the Chinese in the 19th century, it appeared as opium abuse. And among 20th-century Americans, it has occurred as the abuse of crack and cocaine, to name but two problem substances. Whatever the substance of abuse, cultures have had to address the same issue: how to prevent people from misusing mood-altering substances and how to

83

deal with those whose abuse of such substances creates problems for themselves and society.

Societies have approached this problem in two major ways. One has been to pass laws prohibiting or limiting access to drugs and alcohol, so that their scarcity, in combination with the fear of legal punishment, will discourage their use. This can be effective up to a point, but outlawing a particular substance has rarely succeeded in eliminating its use, especially for those who are beyond the point of addiction.

The second approach recognizes substance abuse and addiction as disorders that can be prevented and treated. This way of thinking about addictive behavior is hardly new, but in recent years it has received more attention as a means of addressing the drug problem.

History

Alcohol, besides being the first psychoactive drug to be used by humankind, was also the first to build a record of abuse. "Problem drinking" was recognized as far back as the 1st century B.C. in Rome. Attempts to combat the problem ranged from growing fewer wine grapes to stringing a rope through the noses of excessive drinkers and leading them around in public.

Other cultures that attempted to deal with problem drinking likewise sought to limit access to alcohol (either by prohibition or price increases) or impose penalties on its abusers. Through the ages, alcoholism was widely perceived to be a moral rather than a medical issue. Drinking was a matter of choice, and those who drank excessively had to suffer the consequences.

In 1778, Thomas Trotter, a Scottish physician, wrote one of the earliest discussions of alcoholism as a medical problem. He emphasized that "it is difficult to lay down rules" when dealing with someone who has an alcohol problem and that a good physician must use sensitivity and an understanding of human nature to effectively help the patient. Trotter also referred to alcohol abuse as both a "bodily infirmity" and a "disease of the mind."

Thomas Trotter, a Scottish physician, was one of the first persons to refer to alcohol abuse as both a bodily infirmity and a disease of the mind. Trotter emphasized that in order to deal effectively with alcoholism, a good physician must have sensitivity and an understanding of human nature.

At first, the concept of alcoholism as a disease was not widely accepted, and some medical professionals still disagree with the so-called disease theory of alcoholism. The American Medical Association did not regard alcoholism as a valid medical issue until 1935, and only in 1952 did the World Health Organization officially define alcoholism as a syndrome requiring treatment.

Opiate addiction, although identified earlier than alcoholism, was not seriously researched until the medical use of intravenous morphine became common in the 1870s. At that time, treatment for opiate addiction consisted of little more than helping the addict through the withdrawal process, often using other drugs such as alcohol, barbiturates, and cocaine, along with medical supervision. In his book *The American Disease*, Dr. David Musto notes that from the mid-1800s to the 1920s, most physicians believed that withdrawal and a few weeks of aftercare could effectively cure addiction. Yet research showed that nearly 75% of addicts "cured" in this way went back to using opiates.

Other "cures" for addiction during this era ranged from mail-order patent medicines to expensive, resortlike "hospitals." When the Harrison Act outlawed opiate use without a prescription in 1914, new clinics opened with the sole purpose of dispensing inexpensive opiate drugs to addicts until they could enter a hospital or treatment center. These clinics did little to cure their clients' addiction, and they came to be seen as shady operations run by "dope doctors" looking for big profits, rather than as valid treatment facilities. By 1923, virtually all of them had been outlawed.

While a portion of the medical community had promoted the concept of opiate addiction as a disease, between the late 1800s and early 1900s it also came to be seen, like alcoholism, as a problem of mentally unsound people. In fact, some doctors believed that opiates would produce euphoria only in mentally disordered persons. According to Dr. David Musto, the refusal to define opiate addiction as a disease was probably influenced by a desire to keep opiates illegal. If addiction was a disease, it would be difficult to justify outlawing the drugs that were needed to treat it.

One way in which communities may seek to control substance abuse is by demeaning it, as in this neighborhood billboard-style mural ridiculing the use of crack cocaine.

During the 1930s, a new movement advocated government-run narcotics "farms" to deal with the problem of opiate addiction. This movement arose mainly in response to overcrowding in regular prisons, as well as to complaints that addicts were a bad influence on other prisoners. Since the law defined opiate addicts as criminals, both the Kentucky narcotics farm (opened in 1935) and the Fort Worth narcotics farm (opened in 1938) were basically prisons in which addicts endured the symptoms of withdrawal.

When the trend again shifted toward viewing addiction as a disease in the late 1960s, these prisonlike facilities were reformed. Cells were turned into rooms, and the bars were removed from their windows. The 1960s also saw the birth of community-based treatment programs, in which a number of different strategies were used to help opiate addicts and other drug users. This began the modern era of treatment for substance abuse.

Types of Treatment

Today, various forms of treatment exist for substance abusers. Treatment strategies focus on specific addictions (opiate, cocaine, etc.) and on specific cultural needs based on the ethnic and religious backgrounds of the abusers. The wide range of treatment options is a logical response to the wide range of people who suffer from addictive disorders.

Basically, treatment programs for drug users fall into two categories: outpatient programs and residential treatment programs. Outpatient programs encompass virtually every treatment format in which the patient lives outside the program, ranging from drop-in community groups to highly structured counseling/therapy plans. Residential programs provide a controlled living environment designed to help patients overcome their addiction. This often takes the form of a short-term (generally 30 days or less) detoxification program, usually in a hospital, in which the patient goes through withdrawal and its aftermath under professional medical and psychological care, often followed by a period of outpatient counseling to prevent relapse. By comparison, *therapeutic communities* are essentially group homes in which recovering addicts live together for longer periods (generally 12 to 18 months).

Family involvement is also considered an important element in an addict's recovery, and many programs involve the addict's spouse and children in the treatment process. Often family members need help in dealing with the addict as well as with their own problems. In fact, programs geared specifically toward the needs of the families of substance abusers are now common.

Alcoholics Anonymous and 12-Step Programs

One of the first and most successful forms of outpatient treatment for substance abuse is *Alcoholics Anonymous* (AA). Begun in the mid-1930s by Dr. Robert Smith, a physician, and William Wilson, a stock-broker, AA is a self-help fellowship made up exclusively of alcoholics who are trying to overcome their addiction. By meeting together with other recovering alcoholics and exchanging thoughts and experiences relating to their addiction, participants in AA groups can see that their problems are not unique and receive encouragement from those who have successfully stopped drinking. Strict anonymity is maintained at all times: participants use only their first names, and there is no membership list.

The basic premise of AA is that alcoholism is a disease for which there is no cure—that the alcoholic is forever an alcoholic, even after he or she has stopped drinking (after which the person is said to be in recovery). On this basis, the AA philosophy requires complete abstinence from alcohol, because the alcoholic is considered incapable of moderate or social drinking.

Another aspect of AA is the practice of sponsorship, whereby a long-term AA member makes himself or herself available to a new member for consultation, advice, and emotional support whenever necessary. Participating in an AA group is generally free of cost or has an extremely low cost. Meeting rooms are usually provided free by

The 12 Steps of Alcoholics Anonymous

1. We admitted we were powerless over alcohol—that our lives had become unmanageable.

2. We came to believe that a power greater than ourselves could restore us to sanity.

3. We made a decision to turn our will and our lives over to the care of God as we understood Him.

4. We made a searching and fearless moral inventory of ourselves.

5. We admitted to God, to ourselves, and another human being, the exact nature of our wrongs.

6. We were entirely ready to have God remove all these defects of character.

7. We humbly asked Him to remove our shortcomings.

8. We made a list of all persons we had harmed, and became willing to make amends to them all.

9. We made direct amends to such people whenever possible, except when to do so would injure them or others.

10. We continued to take personal inventory and when we were wrong promptly admitted it.

11. We sought through prayer and meditation to improve our conscious contact with God as we understood Him, praying only for knowledge of His will for us and the power to carry that out.

12. Having had a spiritual awakening as the result of these steps, we tried to carry this message to alcoholics, and to practice these principles in all our affairs.

churches or community organizations, and group expenses (to cover refreshments and other sundries) are generally met by a passing of the hat.

The so-called 12 steps of Alcoholics Anonymous (see page 89) were first outlined by William Wilson in the book *Alcoholics Anonymous* (known to members as the Big Book). The twelve steps describe the key attitudes that AA believes are necessary for recovery from alcoholism. A central element of the twelve steps is a broadly defined spirituality that, while not tied to any specific set of religious beliefs, does require the participant to acknowledge a god or greater power.

A symbolic representation of the 12 steps to surmounting alcoholism established by William Wilson in his book Alcoholics Anonymous. The 12-step approach has become the basis of the behavioral treatment of alcoholism used by Alcoholics Anonymous, the organization founded by Wilson.

To address the needs of those who are uncomfortable with the spiritual element of the traditional program, secular variations of AA, such as Rational Recovery, have been created in recent years. Thus, most people interested in this sort of program can find a group of people with backgrounds similar to their own.

While the religious overtones of 12-step programs, along with their tradition of public confession, have discouraged some persons from participating in them, they have nevertheless flourished. Alcoholics Anonymous has itself grown into an international fellowship with an estimated 800,000 participants in the United States alone. Because of the large number of participants in AA, some regions have groups with a specific orientation toward young people, professionals, women, gays and lesbians, or specific ethnic and religious groups.

The 12-step philosophy has been adapted to a wide variety of addiction treatment and self-help groups, including *Narcotics Anonymous*, which was founded in California in 1953. Similar in concept to AA, Narcotics Anonymous evolved from a recognition of the specific needs of recovering drug abusers and the desire of many AA groups to limit their membership exclusively to alcoholics.

While 12-step programs are among the more popular forms of outpatient treatment for substance abuse, they are certainly not the only option. Many schools and community health centers offer substance abuse counseling on an outpatient basis, and an increasing number of corporate businesses have instituted Employee Assistant Programs (EAPs) that can provide substance abuse counseling and make referrals to other programs. Many private clinics, hospitals, and therapists also deal with addiction problems, using some form of individual, group, or family therapy, along with education about the nature of addictive disorders.

Therapeutic Communities

For some persons with substance abuse problems, outpatient treatment is not sufficient. Homelessness, chronic unemployment, physical and psychiatric disorders, and the absence of a family or support system may all act to perpetuate a person's drug abuse. These people often benefit from a controlled environment in which they can learn how to create a life that does not include drug abuse. *Therapeutic communities* are designed to provide this type of environment.

The very first therapeutic community in the United States was Synanon, established in California in 1958. Synanon was essentially a group home for ex-addicts, many of whom had already gone through federal drug farms or other programs. Based in part on the philosophies of AA, the program was characterized by high-intensity confrontation group therapy in which residents often addressed their problems and grievances by shouting and cursing. Synanon expected its members to adhere to a strict set of rules and regulations; those who did not were either expelled or harshly reprimanded.

The Synanon model evolved into many other therapeutic community-based treatment programs, including Daytop Village and Phoenix House. In general, such programs require the client to make a powerful commitment to treatment, since the latter may take months or even years to complete. They usually provide education and vocational training as a component of their treatment, and many "graduates" of such programs gain employment as counselors in the same communities.

Therapeutic communities generally remain controversial. Critics charge that they do not adequately equip addicts to deal with the outside world, and that the intensity of some programs may create problems with unstable patients. Still, it is clear that therapeutic communities have helped many substance abusers. According to a report issued by the White House in 1988, more than half of all persons undergoing residential treatment for a year or more remain drug-free for at least seven years.

Methadone Maintenance

Although similar to other opiate drugs in most respects (including its ability to produce physical dependence), methadone has certain unique qualities of its own. For example, a patient who is given methadone over a period of time eventually reaches what is called a stabilized

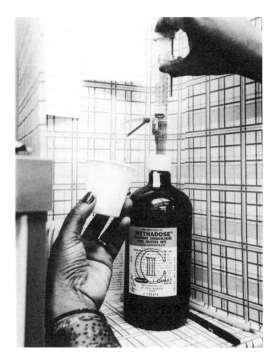

Methadone being dispensed from a container as part of a treatment program for heroin addiction. Such methadone maintenance therapy, in which methadone is given regularly for a long period, helps to end heroin addiction by preventing the withdrawal symptoms that occur when heroin use is stopped.

state, in which the drug no longer produces euphoria but will prevent withdrawal symptoms caused by the discontinuation of other opiates. Furthermore, illicit opiates, such as heroin, will not generally produce euphoria in a patient who has been stabilized on methadone, making addicts undergoing methadone treatment less likely to use these drugs.

The concept of treatment by *methadone maintenance*—providing the opiate addict with a regular, stabilizing dosage of methadone—was first advanced by Drs. Vincent Dole and Marie Nyswander of the Rockefeller University in New York City in 1965. Participants in methadone programs must generally report daily to a clinic, where they receive a single dose of methadone. The drug is usually taken in the form of a soft-drink mixture in the presence of a clinical staff member to ensure that it is not sold or transferred to another person. Some patients may have their dose of methadone gradually reduced over a period of time until they no longer need the drug; others may choose to remain on methadone for an indefinite period.

Dr. Marie Nyswander, who, working with Dr. Vincent Dole during the 1960s, introduced the idea of using methadone to stop heroin addiction.

Methadone maintenance allows a recovering addict to function in a job or school setting without having to turn to illicit narcotics to avoid opiate withdrawal. Methadone treatment also offers addicts the opportunity to stop taking narcotics intravenously, which, as discussed in chapter 6, has been shown to contribute to the spread of AIDS.

Methadone treatment is not without its drawbacks, however. Without proper counseling, methadone maintenance may amount to little more than replacing an old addiction with a new (albeit less problematic) one. And while methadone blocks the euphoric properties of other opiates, it does nothing to discourage the use of nonopiate substances, such as alcohol, barbiturates, tranquilizers, and cocaine. Some critics argue that methadone clinics may even promote the use and sale of other drugs by becoming gathering spots for drug addicts and dealers.

Prevention/Intervention

Because of the hardships and suffering caused by substance abuse and because no treatment methods for it are 100% effective, what makes the most sense is to prevent abuse before it begins. Because research has indicated that the early use of mood-altering substances—especially use before age 15—raises the risk of later substance abuse, most prevention efforts are directed at teenagers.

During the 1960s, most prevention programs sought to discourage drug and alcohol use among youngsters by combining factual information about mood-altering substances with stories designed to instill a fear of their use. Because these messages were often exaggerated, their credibility and effectiveness were limited.

Over the years, research and experience have led to the development of a more varied approach, directed at helping young people to resist pressure from peers and the rest of society to use drugs, alcohol, or tobacco. To help teenagers deal with difficult emotional situations without relying on mood-altering chemicals, school counselors and teachers have been emphasizing communication skills, addressing such specific issues as how to say no and promoting healthy new ways to reduce and cope with stress. A curriculum aimed at increasing self-esteem and clarifying personal values (often referred to as affective education) is included in many drug-abuse prevention programs for young people. Competitive sports, writing, performing and visual arts, participation in drug-free social networks, and hobbies of all sorts are encouraged as positive, creative alternatives to drug use. These activities can increase self-confidence and decrease the alienation and sense of purposelessness that often lead to substance abuse. Experts believe that a comprehensive program should include all of these elements, combined with accurate, credible information about the medical and social consequences of substance abuse.

Intervention, also known as secondary prevention, involves reducing or eliminating the occasional or experimental use of mood-altering substances. Such programs generally consist of the prevention elements already described, along with individual, peer, or group counseling.

Treatment for drug and alcohol abuse has evolved into a multi-million-dollar industry that is not without its critics. Many still hold the old belief of "once an addict, always an addict," labelling hard-core addicts beyond help. Others believe that stiffer legal penalties and increased police efforts are the solution to the nation's drug problems. Many also feel that treating addiction as a disease excuses addicts from taking responsibility for their own condition. Still, although the success of treatment programs is difficult to measure, it is evident that they do aid many people in overcoming substance abuse.

The scope of the drug problem has led many treatment facilities—especially therapeutic communities and methadone programs—to operate beyond their capacities. Many urban programs have waiting lists that range from a few weeks to a few months or more. In fact, although some 4 million Americans had serious drug problems in the late 1980s, according to NIDA, only 800,000 or so received some form of treatment, according to a 1987 White House report. Clearly, if treatment for drug abuse is to make a difference in the "war on drugs," it must be available on demand to all who need it.

CHAPTER 8

PUBLIC POLICY AND THE FUTURE

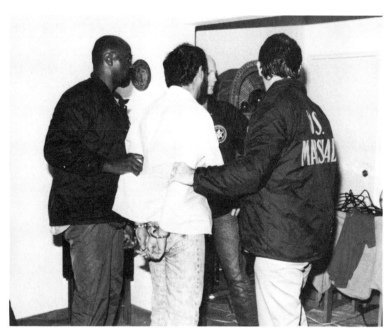

United States marshals arresting a cocaine distributor. Foreign governments have often been reluctant to stop the international distribution of illegal drugs, fearing that they may antagonize their own people in working to solve a domestic problem of the United States.

Since the late 1970s, the rate of substance abuse in the United States has steadily declined, and this trend seems unlikely to change. Yet history shows that the incidence of substance abuse in a society, along with public attitudes toward it, tends to be cyclic, with periods of widespread and accepted (if not condoned) abuse alternating with periods of prohibition and heightened public concern. The constant appearance of new drugs contributes to this phenomenon, changing the economic and cultural patterns of abuse. Thus, when Chinese immigrants introduced opium smoking to the United States in the mid-19th century, it was frowned upon, while at the same time drinking laudanum—an elixir composed of opium and alcohol—was an accepted practice among white middle-class Americans. Similarly, cocaine was primarily a drug of the rich until crack was developed in the early 1980s. While it is difficult to predict the future shape of substance abuse, it is thus unlikely to disappear. The need for new ways of addressing the problem therefore remains.

Can Prohibition Work?

Some sources believe that reducing the supply of mood-altering substances is a more effective answer to abuse than reducing the demand for mood-altering substances through education, prevention, and treatment. Such a strategy may take a variety of forms. Many people insist that the United States, using offers of foreign aid or threats of trade sanctions, must put pressure on foreign governments to attack drug-producing industries within their own borders. These sources also propose that international drug traffickers be captured, turned over to the United States, and tried here so that their maximum punishment is ensured.

A law enforcement officer using a trained dog to detect an illicit drug by its odor. Many persons have urged that international drug traffickers be captured and turned over to the United States for trial and imprisonment.

Eliminating the drug industries of other countries has, however, proven a formidable task. To begin with, it is difficult at best to convince subsistence farmers in South and Central America to stop growing coca plants—the source of cocaine—when this is their only profitable crop. Furthermore, governments are reluctant to enact or enforce laws that may be unpopular in their own countries. They are understandably wary of antagonizing their own people in order to solve the drug-abuse and other domestic problems of such foreign nations as the United States.

This issue becomes even more complicated when one considers that many foreign governments are virtual hostages of the drug cartels that control the multimillion-dollar drug industries in their countries. In Colombia, for instance, the personal risk of speaking or acting against the drug cartels has been well documented; many politicians, judges, lawyers, police officers, and journalists attempting to combat these groups have been murdered. Conversely, those who cooperate with the drug cartels are often rewarded handsomely for their efforts.

Stopping smuggled drugs at the border has been another recommendation for limiting their supply. Such efforts have already had some success; between 1981 and 1986, the amount of cocaine intercepted at America's borders increased from 1.7 to 27.2 metric tons. Yet despite this, the overall amount of cocaine imported into the United States increased during this period. Moreover, the price per kilogram of cocaine fell during the same period from $60,000 to $35,000.

Another effort has been a push toward increasing penalties for individual substance abuse. Thus, William Bennett, former head of the U.S. Drug Enforcement Administration, advocated fines of as much as $10,000 for a drug-abuse infraction. But while this might discourage middle- and upper-class users, it would probably not deter poverty-stricken substance abusers with little in the way of worldly assets. A 1988 report by the Senate Task Force for a Drug-Free America suggested that first-time drug users be made ineligible for welfare and other government entitlement programs and have their driver's licenses revoked and personal assets, such as automobiles, confiscated. But the reality of a costly and already overburdened law enforcement network and an overcrowded national prison system makes this strategy difficult to implement.

By contrast, other sources oppose heavy legal penalties for drug offenders on the grounds that they may increase drug-related violence, including armed resistance to arrest. In fact, arrest may do little to halt illegal drug use. Arrests in Washington, D.C., for illicit drug sales increased from 408 in 1981 to 5,274 in 1986, but the drug market seemed barely affected, as the average cost of drugs on the street reportedly decreased during this period.

Looking back at history, at the Opium Wars between Britain and China, at the bootlegging industry in the United States during Prohibition, and at the current power of the Colombian drug cartels, it seems clear that limiting the sale of mood-altering substances is difficult when it promises huge profits.

The Controversy over Urine Testing

Another recent practice used to reduce the consumption of mood-altering substances has been drug testing, in which a specimen of blood, urine, or another fluid is removed from the body and examined to see if it contains such a substance. Law enforcement agencies, drug treatment centers, sports organizations, and employers have all used this sort of testing—especially the testing of urine, known as *urinalysis*—to uncover drug use by inmates, patients, players, or employees. Urine testing is currently mandatory for employees of the U.S. government and those of many state and local governments. It is also used by about one-fourth of the world's major corporations. According to one survey, most companies will not hire an applicant who has failed a drug test, and one in four will fire an employee who tests positively for drug use.

All of this has raised a number of controversies. One has centered on the accuracy of such tests. Urinalysis, for example, can be done by several different procedures, which vary in terms of their reliability and cost. The least expensive test—radioimmunoassay, or RIA—is also the least reliable. According to some studies, RIA may give false-positive results for cocaine—indicating that the drug is present in the body when it is in fact absent—in as many as 43% of urine samples. More accurate procedures can be so costly that few organizations use them.

A positive test result can mean loss of employment and other damaging consequences for the person tested—certainly inaccuracy in drug testing is thus a legitimate concern. While proponents of testing maintain that all tests for substance abuse are reasonably accurate if administered carefully, the conditions under which they are conducted can vary considerably, and the possibility of human error remains significant.

A further issue in the debate on drug testing is that certain drugs are easier to detect than others. LSD, for example, is virtually undetectable by urinalysis because the dosage in which it is taken is minuscule. Because the body generally eliminates heroin, cocaine, and PCP within two to three days, users of these drugs can often evade detection by temporarily suspending their use of them.

The other big question about drug testing is whether or not it constitutes an invasion of privacy. The fourth amendment to the U.S. Constitution—which guarantees American citizens the right to be "secure in their persons, houses, papers and effects against unreasonable search and seizure"—may preclude urine testing as a form of unreasonable search. But many argue that the danger drug users pose to society—especially if they are persons such as airline pilots or train and bus drivers, who hold human lives in their hands—warrants the broad use of testing.

Drugs and Sports

The tendency of young people to view sports figures as role models has made drug use by athletes a vital social issue. In question here are not only mood-altering drugs but also performance-enhancing drugs, such as stimulants and steroids.

Steroids are synthetic drugs whose effects are similar to those of testosterone, a hormone produced naturally by the male human body. Two kinds of steroids—anabolic or tissue-building steroids, and androgenic steroids, which promote the development of certain male characteristics—are used medically to treat certain nutritional and hormonal disorders. Male and female athletes, however, use steroids to increase their bodies' production of muscle tissue and bone mass, and thus their strength. Steroids often also affect the user psychologically, inducing euphoria, reducing the perception of fatigue, and increasing aggressiveness.

The debate about steroid and stimulant drug use focuses on whether these drugs give an athlete an unfair advantage in competition. Many critics of steroid use, including the American College of Sports Medicine, contend that it does. Others feel that using steroids as part of a controlled, medically supervised training program is no different from taking vitamins.

Another important consideration is the health risk of steroids to their users. High doses of steroids have been linked to liver damage

Shown here as he won the 100-meter race at the 1988 Olympic Summer Games in Seoul, South Korea, Canada's Ben Johnson was later denied the gold medal for the race when it was found that he had used steroids to increase his strength and endurance.

and cardiovascular disease. In women, steroids can disrupt the menstrual cycle and produce male secondary sex characteristics, such as a deepened voice and the growth of facial hair.

Although research on the effects of steroids on athletes is still incomplete, most amateur and professional sports organizations prohibit these drugs and use urine tests to enforce their ruling. Despite this, many athletes continue to use steroids for between-competition training.

The use of mood-altering substances by athletes has been highlighted by the publicity directed at those who are known to have engaged in this practice, such as baseball pitcher Dwight Gooden. Many sports organizations employ urinalysis to detect players' use of such substances, with mandatory suspension of those who test positively.

Legalization and the Future

Though drug use seems to be in decline, a substantial portion of Americans continue to use drugs: nearly 27 million persons—13% of the population—used an illegal drug at least once during the year preceding their participation in the 1990 NIDA Household Survey. According to a survey of chief state and local prosecutors conducted by the *National Law Review* in 1988, more than half felt that the efforts of the criminal justice system were having little or no impact on reducing the use or availability of illegal drugs.

In light of the billions of dollars spent on drug-related law enforcement in the United States each year, some observers have concluded that the costs of fighting the "war on drugs" are too great in terms of both money and personnel. They feel that the war essentially cannot be won and that no amount of law enforcement can stop what has become an estimated $150-billion-a-year business in the United States alone. This view, in turn, has prompted some people to consider the legalization of some or all currently illicit drugs.

Proponents of legalization argue that the legal purchase of drugs would virtually eliminate the illicit drug trade, along with much drug-related crime. Crack cocaine dealers would no longer engage in urban gun battles, and addicts would no longer have to steal to support their drug habits. Organized crime, which may derive more than half its revenues from illicit drug sales, would presumably be dealt a crushing blow. And legalization would probably free billions of law enforcement dollars for use in preventing and treating drug abuse. As a further step, taxing the manufacture and sale of drugs might generate billions of dollars more in revenue. These funds could also be channeled toward drug-rehabilitation and public education programs.

Nevertheless, public opinion seems to be squarely against the idea of legalizing substances of current or potential abuse, and current trends point to an increasing intolerance to drug use of all sorts in the United States. A 1989 Gallup poll indicated that 80% of those surveyed thought complete legalization was a "bad idea," and other polls have found similar opposition, based on concern that legalizing drugs will drastically increase their abuse while sending the message that it is socially acceptable.

Few would argue that substance abuse is a serious problem that affects virtually every society and person—and has done so since the beginning of civilization. The use of mood-altering substances, both legal and illegal, is unlikely to go away. The task ahead, then, is to maintain compassion for those whose use of such substances has brought them and others to harm and to make available a broad range of treatment programs that can assist people in dealing with substance abuse and its related problems. Only in this way will the greatest number of substance abusers be encouraged to seek help.

APPENDIX:
FOR MORE INFORMATION

The following is a list of organizations that can provide information about substance abuse.

GENERAL INFORMATION

Food and Drug Administration
Department of Health and Human
    Services
5600 Fishers Lane
Rockville, MD 20857

ALCOHOL

Addiction Research Foundation
33 Russell Street
Toronto, Ontario M5S 2S1
Canada
(416) 595-6100

Alateen
1372 Broadway
New York, NY 10018
(212) 302-7240

Al-Anon
Family Group Headquarters, Inc.
Box 862, Midtown Station
New York, NY 10018
(212) 302-7240
(For nearest chapter consult your local
    telephone white pages.)

Al-Anon Family Groups (Canada)
National Public Information
P.O. Box 6433, Station "J"
Ottawa, Ontario K2A 3Y6
Canada
(613) 722-1830

Alcohol/Drug Abuse ReferralHotline:
(800) ALC-OHOL
24 hours a day, 7 days a week

Alcoholics Anonymous
475 Riverside Drive
New York, NY 10115
(212) 870-3400

Alcoholics Anonymous
234 Eglinton Avenue East, Suite 502
Toronto, Ontario M4P 1K5
Canada
(416) 487-5591

Canadian Liver Foundation
1320 Yonge Street, Suite 301
Toronto, Ontario M4T 1X2
Canada
(416) 964-1953
(416) 964-0024 (fax)

National Clearinghouse for Alcohol
Information (ONCADI)
P.O. Box 2345
Rockville, MD 20847
(301) 468-2600

National Institute on Alcohol Abuse
and Alcoholism
5600 Fishers Lane
Rockville, MD 20857
(For free booklet, *Communicating with
Youth about Alcohol*, send self-
addressed, stamped envelope.)

DRUG ABUSE

Addiction Research Foundation (see
Alcohol above)
Addicts Anonymous
Box 2000
Lexington, KY 40507

American Council for Drug
Education
204 Monroe Street, Suite 110
Rockville, MD 20850
(301) 294-0600

CareUnit National Treatment System
3156 Glenmore
Cincinnati, OH 45211
(800) 556-CARE

Cocaine Anonymous
World Service Office
Box 1367
Culver City, CA 90239
Hotline (310) 839-1141

Council on Drug Abuse
698 Weston Road, Suite 17
Toronto, Ontario M6N 3R3
Canada
(416) 763-1491
(416) 767-6859 (fax)

Narcotics Anonymous

P.O. Box 9999
Van Nuys, CA 91409
(818) 780-3951

National Clearinghouse for Drug Abuse
Information
11426 Rockville Pike, Suite 200
Rockville, MD 20852
(301) 443-6500

National Hotline for Cocaine Information and Help
P.O. Box 100
Summit, NJ 07902
(800) COCAINE

National Institute on Drug
Abuse (NIDA)
5600 Fishers Lane
Rockville, MD 20857
(800) 662-HELP

Phoenix House Foundation
164 West 74th Street
New York, NY 10023
(212) 595-5810

PRIDE Canada
(Parent Resources Institute for Drug
Education)
College of Pharmacy
University of Saskatchewan
Saskatoon, Saskatchewan S7N 0W0
Canada
(306) 975-3755
(800) 667-3747

Straight, Inc.
3001 Gandy Blvd.
St. Petersburg, FL 33702
(813) 576-8929

Target—Helping Students Cope with
Alcohol and Drugs
P.O. Box 20626

Kansas City, MO 64195
(816) 464-5400

SMOKING

American Cancer Society
19 West 56th Street
New York, NY 10019
(212) 586-8700

American Lung Association
National Headquarters
1740 Broadway
New York, NY 10019
(212) 315-8700

Canadian Council on Smoking and
  Health
1565 Carling Avenue, Suite 400

Ottawa, Ontario K1Z 8R1
Canada
(613) 722-3419
(613) 725-9826 (fax)

Canadian Lung Association
75 Albert Street, Suite 908
Ottawa, Ontario K1P 5E7
Canada
(613) 237-1208
(613) 563-3362 (fax)

Smoking and Health Action Foundation
344 Bloor Street West, Suite 308
Toronto, Ontario M5S 3A7
Canada
(416) 928-2900
(416) 928-1860 (fax)

FURTHER READING

Abadinsky, Howard. *Drug Abuse: An Introduction*. Chicago: Nelson-Hall, 1989.

Al-Anon's Twelve Steps And Twelve Traditions. New York: Al-Anon Family Group Headquarters, 1983.

Byrd, Oliver E. *Medical Readings on Drug Abuse*. Reading, MA: Addison-Wesley, 1970.

Cahalan, Don. *Understanding America's Drinking Problem*. San Francisco: Jossey-Bass, 1987.

Cohen, Sidney. *The Substance Abuse Problems*. New York: Haworth Press, 1981.

Drug Abuse and Drug Abuse Research: The Third Triennial Report to Congress. Rockville, MD: U.S. Department of Health and Human Services, 1991.

Friedman, Alfred S., and George M. Beschner, eds. *Treatment Services for Adolescent Substance Abusers*. Rockville, MD: U.S. Department of Health and Human Services, 1985.

Gold, Mark S. *The Facts About Drugs and Alcohol*. New York: Bantam, 1988.

Hart, Stan. *Rehab*. New York: HarperCollins, 1988.

Hughes, Barbara. *Drug-Related Diseases.* New York: Franklin Watts, 1987.

Milkman, Harvey B., and Howard J. Shaffer, eds. *The Addictions: Multidisciplinary Perspectives and Treatments.* Lexington, MA: Lexington Books, 1985.

Musto, David F. *The American Disease: Origins of Narcotic Control.* New York: Oxford University Press, 1987.

Peele, Stanton. *The Meaning of Addiction.* Lexington, MA: Lexington Books, 1985.

Serban, George. *Social and Medical Aspects of Drug Abuse.* New York: Spectrum, 1984.

Washton, Arnold M., and Donna Boundy. *Cocaine and Crack: What You Need To Know.* Hillside, NJ: Enslow, 1989.

Yoder, Barbara. *The Recovery Resource Book.* New York: Simon & Schuster, 1990.

Zinberg, Norman E., and Wayne M. Harding, eds. *Control over Intoxicant Use.* New York: Human Sciences Press, 1983.

GLOSSARY

abstinence syndrome a set of psychological and physical symptoms that occur when the use of an addictive substance is suddenly stopped

addiction an uncontrollable compulsion to use a drug or other substance

AIDS acquired immune deficiency syndrome; an acquired weakening of the immune system, thought to be caused by the HIV virus and spread by exchange of body fluids such as blood, semen, and vaginal secretions. It leaves people vulnerable to fatal infections and cancers

Alcoholics Anonymous a self-help fellowship begun in the United States during the mid-1930s in which recovering alcoholics meet regularly in groups to offer support and consolation to one another while working to overcome their addictions

amphetamines a group of stimulant drugs sometimes prescribed for use in weight loss

anesthetic an agent that diminishes or eliminates sensation

barbiturates a group of depressant drugs that are often prescribed by doctors to treat sleeplessness

basuco a smokable paste that contains cocaine and toxic substances such as gasoline or kerosene

biopsychosocial model a theory that addiction is caused by the interaction of biological, psychological, and social factors within an individual

caffeine a stimulant found in coffee, tea, and other sources that has been shown to produce both physical and psychological dependence in users

Cannabis/Cannabis sativa the plant from which marijuana is obtained; also, marijuana itself

central nervous system (CNS) specifically, the brain and spinal cord, which together are responsible for the integration of all nervous activities

chasing the dragon slang for smoking heroin

cocaine babies infants who are born—often with a variety of health problems—to mothers who have used cocaine in one form or another during their pregnancy

crack a smokable form of cocaine

crash various substances used to dilute the purity of a drug, generally for the purpose of increasing its mass or value; also, the act of diluting a drug

depressant a substance that reduces the activity of a body system or function, especially the central nervous system

detoxification the process of completely ridding the body of a particular substance or substances

disease theory of addiction a theory that holds that addiction fits many of the criteria used to define other diseases and should therefore be treated as a disease

drug cartels large-scale criminal organizations that deal in illicit drugs

drug prevention strategies for discouraging the use of mood-altering substances, generally aimed at young persons who have not yet experimented with such substances

ecstasy one of a group of potent stimulants that produce euphoria and a heightened sense of closeness to other persons

Erythroxylon coca the plant from which cocaine is derived

euphoria a feeling of optimism, cheerfulness, and well-being

fetal alcohol syndrome a disorder that afflicts infants whose mothers have consumed alcohol during pregnancy. It may be characterized by a variety of physical and mental deficiencies

freebasing the process of converting cocaine into a smokable form; also, the act of smoking the product of freebasing

ganja marijuana

genetic predisposition an inherited tendency; one explanation for addictive behavior

hallucinogen a substance that can produce hallucinations, such as LSD or peyote

hashish a concentrated form of marijuana which usually takes the form of a light- or dark-brown, puttylike mass

hash oil a smokable, highly concentrated resinous extract of the marijuana plant

hemp the fibrous material found in the stalk and branches of the *Cannabis* plant, which also produces marijuana. Hemp has historically been used for making rope, paper, and other products; also, the plant itself

hypodermic a type of syringe tipped with a thin, hollow needle used for injecting substances beneath the skin

ice a smokable form of amphetamine

intervention strategies for discouraging and reducing the use of mood-altering substances in persons who are occasional users of these substances, especially alcohol

intoxication symptoms produced by the ingestion of mood-altering substances, especially alcohol

intravenous (IV) drug use a method of administering drugs, usually involving the use of a hypodermic needle, in which a drug is injected directly into a vein or artery

lysergic acid diethylamide-25 (LSD) a powerful hallucinogenic substance derived from the ergot fungus found on rye and other grasses

magic mushrooms mushrooms that contain the hallucinogen psilocybin

MDMA (Methylenedioxymethamphetamine) also called ecstasy, a potent psychoactive drug chemically related to the amphetamines

metabolism the biochemical processes that transform one substance into another within the body

methadone maintenance a form of treatment for opiate—mainly heroin—addiction that entails giving the patient regular doses of methadone to prevent withdrawal symptoms

morphine an opiate drug commonly prescribed as a painkiller

narcotic opiate; often used incorrectly as a blanket term for illicit drugs

National Institute on Drug Abuse (NIDA) the main federal agency for research into the prevalence of drug abuse, its causes, and approaches to its prevention and treatment

nicotine a mood-altering alkaloid, derived from tobacco, that has been shown to produce both physical and psychological dependence in tobacco smokers

opiate any drug derived from the dried juice of the opium poppy; also, a synthetic drug with a chemical similarity to true opiates

outpatient treatment any of a number of types of drug-abuse treatment programs that allow patients to live on their own while undergoing treatment

PCP (phencyclidine) a powerful drug that can manifest the characteristics of hallucinogens, sedatives, or stimulants

peyote the fleshy center or "button" of the peyote cactus, that contains mescaline, a powerful hallucinogenic substance

physical dependence a state of adaptation to a substance, characterized by the development of tolerance to the substance's effects and withdrawal symptoms when use of the substance is stopped

Prohibition the period from 1920 to 1933 in American history, during which the use and sale of alcohol was outlawed in the United States

psilocybin a powerful hallucinogen that occurs naturally in a variety of wild mushrooms that grow throughout different parts of the world

psychoactive affecting the mind, specifically sensory processes, emotions, and behavioral responses

psychological dependence an overwhelming desire to repeat the use of a particular substance to produce pleasure or avoid discomfort

rebound the period during which the body attempts to readjust to normal function after the effects of a mood-altering substance have worn off

sedatives drugs that produce calmness, relaxation, and, in high doses, sleep; includes barbiturates

speedball a combination of heroin and cocaine that is usually injected into a vein by intravenous drug users

steroids usually two specific kinds of synthetic substances, anabolic and androgenic, that closely resemble testosterone—the male sex hormone. They are used by athletes to increase body strength and tissue mass

stimulant a substance that provokes the activity of a body system or function, especially the central nervous system

substance abuse any use of a mood-altering substance that endangers the health and well-being of the user and those in contact with the abuser

therapeutic community (TC) a type of substance abuse treatment in which the patient lives with other recovering substance abusers in a controlled, group-home setting

tolerance the need to progressively increase the dosage of a substance in order to achieve the effects that were once produced by a smaller dose

12-step program an addiction-rehabilitation program based on the "12 steps," or key attitudes, that Alcoholics Anonymous considers essential for control of alcoholism

urine testing the chemical analysis of urine to detect traces of illicit drugs in the body

withdrawal syndrome the physical and psychological symptoms that occur when an addictive substance is abruptly discontinued

INDEX

Smith, Robert, 88
Snorting, 64
Snuff, 26
Sodium pentothal, 39
Spacebasing, 66
Speakeasies, 31
Speed. *See* Amphetamines
Speedballing, 66
Steroids, 101–3
    health risks, 102–3
Stimulants, 14–15, 43–46. *See also* Amphetamines
Substance abuse. *See also* specific substances
    addiction, 19–21
    biopsychosocial model, 19–21
    death and, 22
    as disease, 21–22
    legalization and, 103–4
    pregnancy and, 24, 29, 69, 78
    public policy and, 97–101
    reasons for substance use, 14–16
    rehabilitation, 83–96
        in history, 84–87
        prevention/intervention, 22–23, 95–96
        sports and, 101-3
        types of treatment, 87–94
Sufi, 50
Sumerians, 73
Synanon, 92
Synesthesia, 55

Talcum powder, 61, 78
Tardive dyskensia, 43
Temperance movement. *See* Prohibition
Thailand, 72
Thea sinensis, 29
Therapeutic communities, 87–88, 91–92
Thioridazine, 42
Thorazine, 42
Tibet, 50

Tobacco, 26–28. *See also* Cigarette smoking
    deaths related to, 22
    historical use, 26
    origin of name, 26
    properties, 26
    source, 26
    withdrawal symptoms, 27
Tofranil, 43
Tolerance, 19
Tranquilizers, 15, 41–42, 94
Trotter, Thomas, 84
Tuinal, 39
Turkey, 26, 51
Twenty-first Amendment, 31

Ulcers, 33
Urinalysis, 100–1

Valium, 41
Vasoconstriction, 61
Ventricular fibrillation, 68
Ventricular tachycardia, 68
Verne, Jules, 62
Vietnam War, 20, 56
Virginia, 26

Washington, D.C., 100
Washton, Arnold, 22
West Indies, 26
Whippets, 36
Wilson, William, 88, 90
Window pane, 54
Wine, 15
Withdrawal syndrome, 19
Wood, Alexander, 75
World Health Organization, 85
World War II, 45, 81

Xylocaine, 60

Young, Francis, 52

PICTURE CREDITS

William Hermes is a teacher and a freelance writer who has developed substance abuse educational materials for the New York City Board of Education and the New York State Division of Substance Abuse. He received a bachelor's degree in English from the State University of New York at Binghamton and a master's degree in education from Queens College in Queens, New York. He currently lives in Minneapolis, Minnesota.

Dale C. Garell, M.D., is medical director of California Children Services, Department of Health Services, County of Los Angeles. He is also associate dean for curriculum at the University of Southern California School of Medicine and clinical professor in the Department of Pediatrics & Family Medicine at the University of Southern California School of Medicine. From 1963 to 1974, he was medical director of the Division of Adolescent Medicine at Children's Hospital in Los Angeles. Dr. Garell has served as president of the Society for Adolescent Medicine, chairman of the youth committee of the American Academy of Pediatrics, and as a forum member of the White House Conference on Children (1970) and White House Conference on Youth (1971). He has also been a member of the editorial board of the *American Journal of Diseases of Children.*

C. Everett Koop, M.D., Sc.D., is former Surgeon General, deputy assistant secretary for health, and director of the Office of International Health of the U.S. Public Health Service. A pediatric surgeon with an international reputation, he was previously surgeon-in-chief of Children's Hospital of Philadelphia and professor of pediatric surgery and pediatrics at the University of Pennsylvania. Dr. Koop is the author of more than 175 articles and books on the practice of medicine. He has served as surgery editor of the *Journal of Clinical Pediatrics* and editor-in-chief of the *Journal of Pediatric Surgery.* Dr. Koop has received nine honorary degrees and numerous other awards, including the Denis Brown Gold Medal of the British Association of Paediatric Surgeons, the William E. Ladd Gold Medal of the American Academy of Pediatrics, and the Copernicus Medal of the Surgical Society of Poland. He is a chevalier of the French Legion of Honor and a member of the Royal College of Surgeons, London.